Life in Beauty

Life in Beauty

Kate Porter

 Granville Island Publishing

Library and Archives Canada Cataloguing in Publication

Porter Kathleen J., 1946-
    Life in beauty / Kathleen (Kate) J. Porter.
ISBN 978-1-894694-66-7
1. Aesthetics. 2. Inspiration. 3. Affirmations. I. Title.

BJ1595.P67 2008   158.1   C2007-907673-4

Author Photo: Bodhi Drope
Editor: Gordon Thomas
Proofreading: Kyle Hawke
Book Interior Design: Kate Moore and Laura Kinder
Cover and Box Design: Marya Zubaty

www.lifeinbeauty.com

First Edition

Granville Island Publishing
212-1656 Duranleau
Vancouver, BC
V6H 3S4
1-877-688-0320
www.granvilleislandpublishing.com

Printed in China

Contents

Introduction

This is a book about beauty — what it is, how it affects us, where we find it, how to bring it into our lives and why we might want to do that.

The initial inspiration to write *Life in Beauty* came to me two years ago at a seminar I was attending. As I walked along the back of the room to find my seat, I looked up and had a vision of myself on the stage talking about beauty. In that moment, my life changed. So many of my life experiences fell into place and I knew what my work over the next few decades was to be. I turned to my husband and said, "I have to write a book about beauty and then I have to talk about it." He laughed at me. That didn't matter. I instinctively knew what I was called to do.

A week later, my marriage of twenty-four years collapsed. In ten days, I was to turn fifty-nine years old. I decided that if the rest of my life was going to be spent alone, I had better get on with it, as I was about to begin my sixtieth year on my own. So, two days before my fifty-ninth birthday, I moved into a two-room apartment. One room was my studio and the other was my living space. I was beginning a two-year inner journey that culminated in this book.

The first few months in my new apartment were filled with self-reflection. No matter what my husband had done, I knew that there had been two of us in the relationship and, in some way, I was complicit in the failure of the marriage. I had three major supports during this intense period: my yoga teacher Brett, my spiritual advisor Tracy and a book entitled *A Course in Miracles*. The second day I was installed in my apartment, (which also happened to be my birthday) I did the first meditation in the *Course*. I have consistently studied this profound text ever since.

There were many days when I did absolutely nothing. I would get out of bed, do 40 minutes of yoga, meditate, prepare and eat breakfast. Then I would sit, listen to music and gaze out the front window. I do not recall if I even thought about anything.

I just looked outside.

I did this hour after hour. I was still in shock, for I had always thought I would grow old with my husband. However, I was determined to heal myself. For me, quiet time alone was a necessity. That is not to say that I was completely alone. My family and my friends were wonderful to me. My children called or visited, my mother kept tabs on me, and my friends never allowed me to go too long without contact. I recall one day, sitting in my studio thinking, "I need to talk to somebody." Immediately, the telephone rang and a girl-friend I hadn't spoken to in over a year was on the line. She was just making sure I was okay.

All through my healing, things like that happened. People would suddenly show up just when I needed them. During this period, I managed to maintain my business, although I cannot remember anything about the day-to-day activities I engaged in. I know I made and shipped jewelry because I have the receipts to prove it, but I remember virtually nothing about it. I am still fascinated by what we are capable of doing while experiencing painful personal loss.

Six months later, I was much better. Interestingly, my mother was also alone at this time as my father, suffering from de-mentia, had been placed in a nursing home three months before my marriage broke up. Though she would have happily taken me in to live with her when I left my husband, I knew that was not an option. I needed some time to myself. Even so, six months after my separation, I began thinking that if we pooled our resources we could find a wonderful place to live. Within a week, we found the perfect home and I began looking for a studio. That too showed up just as easily, and a new and beautiful life began for me.

Still, I did not write about beauty. I thought about it a great deal, registered some domain names for a website, developed ideas for a beauty business and even spoke with a management consultant. But not a word was written. Instead, I decorated my home and my studio.

I enjoyed the summer in my studio, exhibited my jewelry at trade shows and still didn't write anything of any significance. Not until I decided to devote a day a week to writing did anything of consequence happen and that began shortly after I got my divorce. As soon as I made that commitment to myself and organized my life accordingly, my world changed. Out of nowhere people showed up, telling

me their stories about beauty. New friends entered my life and it was them I talked to about my project, rather than my oldest and dearest friends. I cannot really explain why this happened but I have learned that one needs to accept what shows up and go with it.

Projects such as this are rarely solo efforts. I am grateful to many people who have generously offered their support. First of all, I want to thank all the wonderful people who shared their stories of beauty with me. They were instrumental in helping me understand what beauty is and where to find it. Throughout the writing of the book, my mother has been a steady support. She has read every version of the book and has always believed in it. Tracy, Dorothy, Jen and Mary Lu all read the manuscript and all have contributed to its accuracy. My editor Gordon, in the gentlest of ways, has challenged me and made the work worthwhile. And finally, there is my very dear friend, Art, who never once forgot to ask "How is your project coming?" Thank you all.

The Experience of Beauty

Far away there in the sunshine are my highest aspirations. I may not reach them, but I can look up and see their beauty, believe in them and try to follow where they lead.

— Louisa May Alcott

We all know beauty. Each one of us has personally experienced it. In our minds, in our hearts, in our spirits and even in our bodies, we recognize it when we see it. Perhaps we were walking along the beach after a rain shower and looked up to see a double rainbow in the sky. Perhaps we were visiting an art gallery and saw a wonderful sculpture that seemed to draw us into it. Perhaps we heard a piece of music that filled us with joy. Perhaps we watched an athlete perform some amazing feat of strength. Perhaps we witnessed a young mother cuddling her child. Beauty is everywhere: above us, below us, around us and inside us.

No matter what or how we experience beauty, we all have a similar response to it. An *aha* of sorts occurs and for a moment the mundane patterns of our life, our thoughts and actions are interrupted as we experience something beautiful. Often we are so taken by the moment that we invite others into our experience. "Look," we might say, "look at the eagle flying across the harbor." They look up and together, in silence, watch the bird make its way across the sky.

This is a different kind of sharing from discussing a problem with a co-worker or a spouse. Such discussions can be intense and even riveting, but the experience of beauty is completely different, for rather than drawing us into the problems of life, it takes us out of them. Instead of frustration, concern, intensity, confusion, worry or challenge, we experience awe, wonder and joy. Isn't it interesting then that we do not in our day-to-day lives consider beauty to be important? Instead, we assign importance to the frustrations of life.

The Importance of Beauty

*B*eauty inspires. But how exactly does it inspire and why would that be so? To answer that question, I must recount an experience I had some twenty-five years ago, one that to this day is still with me.

I was traveling in Italy. While in Florence, I got up early one morning in order to visit the Accadamia before the crowds arrived. At 8:30 a.m., I arrived within sight of the building. Just ahead of me, a tour bus pulled in and out of it climbed thirty American tourists. I remember

wishing they had been German or French or Russian, because I could understand Americans and I was certain they would distract me and interrupt my experience. Nevertheless, I followed the bevy of tourists into the building. We were all there to see the most famous sculpture in the world, Michelangelo's David.

When I first entered the Accadamia, I encountered a cavernous room full to overflowing with sculpture. It was absolutely overwhelming. Like everyone else, I moved from one piece of art to the next, astonished at the sheer number, not to mention range of pieces. The incessant chatter of tourists was annoying but the art was gorgeous and somehow I was able to ignore their comments. I eventually moved out of that room and made a left turn into yet another full of magnificent sculpture. I made my way through it and then took a right turn. I was in a long vaulted corridor. Some fifty yards ahead, I could see David standing on a pedestal in a rotunda under a skylight.

Not two weeks before, I had been in the Louvre in Paris looking at the Mona Lisa. The room was crowded with visitors. There was lots of chatter and one could only get a glimpse of the famous painting. It was an enormous disappointment. My experience in Florence, however, was completely different.

As I moved along the corridor towards the sculpture, conversation among the tour group gradually subsided. When we finally stood beside David, we were speechless. Occasionally one person would connect with another. When he or she did so, it was in a whisper. It was amazing, similar to being in church, for the silence was imbued with reverence.

For many years thereafter, I would recall the experience with David. And I would wonder what happened. Why was it that everyone was silent in the presence of this piece of art?

James Joyce would take the position that this is "proper art," for the observer is thrown into a state of silence. If art thrusts the viewer into action, according to Joyce, the piece is

improper art. Proper art stops the observer such that he says nothing, does nothing. This is also what occurs in the presence of beauty. Why is that so? What causes us to stop what we are doing and thinking to watch the beauty of the eagle flying across the harbor?

While I was happy with Joyce's explanation, I continued to wonder why the silence happened. What is it about beauty that causes that? I found an explanation in a most unexpected place: the Native American Medicine Wheel.

I have been aware of the Medicine Wheel for many years through my Cree and Ojibway friends. In addition, my great-grandmother was Cree. And while my friends would say that all of life is on the Medicine Wheel, for the longest time I couldn't figure out what they were talking about

Eventually, a teacher explained it to me in a way that I could understand. She explained that the Medicine Wheel is comprised of the four directions and that each direction is symbolic of the four attributes that constitute the human experience. As she put it, "In the West sits the heart; in the East sits the mind; in the South sits the body; in the North sits the spirit." So, according to her, the attributes of humanity are heart, mind, body and spirit.

East/West Axis	North/South Axis
Mind/Heart	*Spirit/Body*
Past/Future	Present
Activity	Action
Mundane	Magic
Suffering	Joy
Left Brain	Right Brain
Innovation	Creativity
Fear	Love
Anger	Forgiveness
Greed	Gratitude
Busy-ness	Being
Protective	Open
Control	Power
Judgment	Acceptance
Unconscious patterned behavior	Conscious present behavior

Thus the cornerstones of humanity are mind, heart, body and spirit. It is how these act on the axes of the medicine wheel that explains how beauty works. The East/West axis is the axis through which we experience our day-to-day life. It is where we take out the garbage, do the dishes, attend meetings, talk on the telephone, drive to work, visit the dentist and so on. It is the activities of daily life, the activities which take up most of our time and attention. In fact, for many of us, it is what we think of as life. It is our life in time, the life of objectives and deadlines, of plans and dreams, of successes and failures. Life on the East/West axis is life in time. It is life on the surface.

The North/South axis is the axis through which we experience joy and wonder. Sometimes it is intensely physical engagement such as that an athlete achieves. Or it might be complete immersion in a creative project. Or it might be making love. Whatever the action, the common experience is one of timelessness, of time standing still and of a profound sense of silence either in the experience or immediately following it. Life on the North/South axis is life out of time. It is life in depth. And beauty can take us there.

If there are four cornerstones of humanity, it makes sense that we ought to be able to experience all cornerstones in equal measure. And yet this is not how our lives are structured. Contemporary Western life is largely structured to accent the horizontal axis. The vertical axis is given only passing attention. And yet, if the Medicine Wheel is correct, the vertical axis is where creativity and true power reside. In times of enormous change such as we are currently experiencing, it seems to me that we need to pay attention to depth in life and perhaps lighten up a little on breadth.

This is the primary importance of beauty. It takes us off the horizontal axis out of the mundane and onto the vertical axis into joy. We move from busy-ness to being, from control to power.

Life on the East/West axis is largely visible. It takes place in real time and it can be measured. It has a kind of distance to it. It is often lived out of memory. Life on the North/South axis, on the other hand, is immediate and fleeting, almost invisible. Rather than having distance, it has depth. Rather than having history, experience on body/spirit axis occurs in the moment, in the now.

On the one hand, experience on the North/South axis occurs in the moment and on the other, it seems like only a moment. I am reminded of a conversation I had with a woman who had just become a mother for the first time. She had a long and difficult labor and delivery of over thirty hours. But when she told me about it, the time had no relevance to her. "I was in it," she said to me. "I didn't notice how much time was passing." From the point of view of the East/West axis, it is hard to imagine that thirty hours was not noticeable. However, pay attention to her words: "I was in it." There is no separation. As the experience is described, it is described in terms of depth. This is the essential experience of the body/spirit continuum. It has depth to it.

Everyone who saw Michelangelo's David on the day I was there had that same experience. We were, in a sense, *in* the sculpture. There was no separation. No mind entered to describe it to us. We were there. And when we are absolutely present, the natural state is one of silence. But it is not an external silence. It is an inner silence. That is, it is a silence that is generated from within. The mind stops its incessant chattering and we fully experience what is before us.

Ohiyesa describes it this way:

The first American . . . believes profoundly in silence — the sign of perfect equilibrium. Silence is the absolute poise or balance of body, mind and spirit. The man who preserves his selfhood is ever calm and unshaken by the storms of existence — not a leaf, as it were, astir on the tree; not a ripple upon the surface of the shining pool — his, in the mind of the unlettered sage, is the ideal attitude and conduct of life.

If you ask him: "What is silence?" he will answer: "It is the Great Mystery!" "The holy silence is His voice!" If you ask: "What are the fruits of silence?" he will say: "They are self-control, true courage or endurance, patience, dignity, and reverence. Silence is the cornerstone of character."

Silence brings forth truth. My father was an excellent interrogator. He was a police detective and when there was a complex interrogation to be done he would be called in to lead the interrogation. His secret was silence. He did not, as we often see in movies, browbeat or threaten his subjects. He simply patiently waited in silence. He was a man of immense presence, of considerable integrity and of few words. That combination inevitably brought the truth forward.

But he did not live in silence alone, although he never talked about his work. He would come home, have dinner with us and catch up on family news. Then he would go downstairs to his workshop and build something out of wood. This bringing something into the physical out of a place of silence is profoundly important in keeping in touch with the vertical axis. It is why proper art is so important to us. And it is why paying attention to beauty matters.

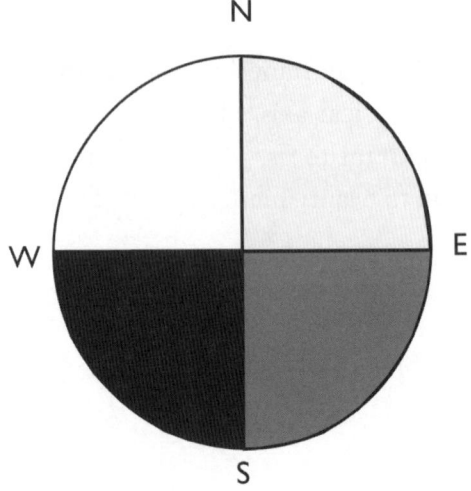

Medicine Wheel

Learning Beauty

If beauty is really that important, where do we learn it? How do we come to know beauty in our lives? My guess is that we know it already. What seems to happen is we unlearn beauty as we grow up. Perhaps you have had the privilege of being beside a three-year-old child as he wakes up in the morning. One moment he is sleeping and the next, his eyes are wide open and he is ready to embrace the day. And I mean embrace. Young children are thrilled to wake up in the morning. They know life is wonderful and they are excited and enthusiastic about experiencing it. This is their natural state. We as their elders have the opportunity to encourage this experience or threaten it.

When my son was two years old, he was entranced by my mother's collection of Royal Doulton figurines. He loved them and wanted to touch them. My mother would put him on her knee, pick up a figurine and give it to him to hold. They would talk about how beautiful it was. My mother would explain to him that this was a fragile object and that because of that it needed to be cared for and treasured. After they had inspected the piece, my son would very carefully replace it on the table. Then he would jump down off my mother's knee and would proceed to play with his cars. If he wanted to touch a figurine, he would ask his grandmother to help him. Though today he is not interested in Royal Doulton, he does have many objects in his home that are treated with care and placed in such a way as to indicate how they are treasured.

On the other hand, I watched the following occur with a child in my extended family. He was about eleven months old, just pulling himself up into a standing position, leaning on anything that was handy. While I was visiting, he pulled himself up and leaned against the coffee table. He noticed a beautiful bowl on the table and being naturally curious, he leaned forward to touch it. His father immediately slapped his hand and shouted "No!" At a very young age he learned that objects of beauty which attracted him were not to be experienced. Indeed, participation with them resulted in pain. I have even heard of children who have been beaten for touching fragile objects. In one case, the child touched a Royal Doulton figurine.

Here are two similar circumstances. The objects in question are both treasured. In each situation, the children learn that beautiful things are to be valued. However the imprints relating to them are direct opposites. In the one case, beautiful things can be touched and admired. In the other case, beautiful things are to be feared.

Let me offer a second example. When my children were in grade school, I was studying classical guitar. My youngest son was fascinated by this instrument so he started lessons with my teacher as well. My teacher's wife was, at that time, learning to play the saxophone and our boy heard her playing. He said, "What is that?" Our teacher answered, "My wife is playing the saxophone." He then took my stepson into meet her and to see the saxophone. Well, he wanted to do that. That was the instrument for him. He was told that he was still too small to play one and that he needed to be eleven or twelve to be strong enough to hold the instrument. Being mindful of his response, when he was twelve, we found a saxophone teacher for him. Suffice it to say that today he is a professional musician, his instrument of choice being the baritone sax.

On the other hand, I recall a conversation with a woman whose son was in the same sixth-grade class as my second son. She wanted her son to play violin. So, she started him in classes. He wanted to play the drums. "Well," she told me, "I am not putting up with all that racket." Then, in the next breath, she bemoaned the fact that he wouldn't practice the violin. She could not make the connection between the importance of her son's desires versus her desires. One child learned to love to play music while the other learned to hate to play music. My guess is that that is the normal case for learning about beauty. Mostly what happens is we unlearn it.

In "Left Brain : Right Brain" [1], author Dan Eden points out that before children attend school, they test as highly creative. By age seven, only 10% of children test as highly creative. By the time they reach adulthood, the results are even worse. Only two percent of adults test as highly creative. This

[1] "Left Brain : Right Brain", Dan Eden, www.viewzone.com/bicam.html

occurs because most of what is emphasized in schools are the cognitive skills of reading, writing, arithmetic and memorization. If we believe that humans are made up of mind, heart, body and spirit, then it seems odd that we address only one aspect of humanity in our school system. It is, of course, not at all odd if one considers that the public school system was designed to graduate compliant citizens and good factory workers who could take orders and behave like machines in their work. Naturally, one does not address heart, body or spirit if that is the desired result.

To invite beauty into our lives, we have to trust our instincts and pay attention to our experience. If we can stop long enough, we can hear what makes our spirit sing. And what makes your spirit sing is not necessarily what makes mine sing. For example, I have a favorite painting. If you ask me, I can name it. I have never even seen it in real life. I went all the way to the Uffizi Gallery in Florence to see it and that particular summer it was away being restored. That painting, is Botticelli's *Annunciation*. When I read about the painting I read about the unusual arabesque that Mary is performing in the piece, its intriguing background, the rich colors and how the robes flow. But none of these things matter to me. Somehow, the painting touches me deeply — beyond words, beyond feeling. There is some truth in it with which I resonate. Is this the best painting in the world? Of course not. It is just my favorite. Your favorite painting is most probably something else. And that is right for you.

Beauty is a deeply personal matter. And it is a matter worth attending. I think of the great Brazilian soccer player Pelé. He calls the game he plays so well "the beautiful game." He doesn't call it a great game. He calls it beautiful. Now, here is a man who knows how to be 'in the game'. He plays with dignity, grace and beauty. Can there be anything better?

Integrating Beauty

Of course, what Pelé experiences in playing football is deeply physical. Given that the root of the North/South axis is the physical, it is not surprising that he experiences beauty in what he does, for the action of playing football can take him to the silence of spirit. But notice that getting to beauty is an action. It is a doing. It is an experience into which one must enter. It is something we choose.

As I was learning about my Cree heritage, I became fascinated and moved by the richness of utilitarian objects. Bows and arrows, of course, were fashioned by hand. A hunter made his own bow and then imbued it with spirit. He might carve the symbol for the wind or for the hunter. These spirits assisted him when he went out to hunt for his village. A woman might carve a basket to be used for gathering berries. Embedded in the basket would be patterns and symbols intended to depict a plentiful harvest; perhaps the spirit of the harvest would be woven into the object. A great deal of care was taken in the creation of these objects so that life on the East/West axis was imbued with spirit from the North/South axis. Day-to-day objects are made beautiful by inflection with spirit.

This is not the case with the myriad of objects which populate my life. As long as something has a practical purpose, that is enough. People choose telephones for their usefulness and it never occurs to them that, perhaps, the spirit of communication could be embossed on the receiver so that we might be reminded of right speaking. Nor do I see the spirit of the harvest carved into the wood on my pepper mill. Our culture measures value according to time and utility, both attributes of the axis of the mundane.

There is a famous comment made by William Morris that is frequently quoted whenever the question of beauty is raised. Morris states, "Have nothing in your houses that you do not know to be useful, or believe to be beautiful." What is interesting about this is that the assumption behind it is that beauty and utility are separate things. And certainly, if we look at the idea of the two axes of humanity, it can be seen that way. Beauty belongs on the North/South axis and utility belongs on the East/West. But notice that my Cree ancestors combined utility and beauty. A carved bowl to gather berries is profoundly useful while the carvings on it are profoundly beautiful. The idea then, is not to separate beauty from our lives but to integrate it.

All four attributes of humanity are equally important. Heart, mind, body and spirit all matter.

Unfortunately, Western life has separated the attributes and tends to inflect the mind/heart axis so that the body/spirit axis is set aside. This has happened in two ways — one a matter of perception and the other a matter of spiritual guidance.

Language and Beauty

*O*ur perceptions are largely channeled through language. We describe our experience first to ourselves and then to others with words. The grammar of Indo-European English is divided by time (past, present, future) and by gender (masculine, feminine, neuter). This is so deeply imbedded in my language that I think of it as true. I forget that these divisions were invented by the human mind. They are not a universal truth and they condition my experience of reality if I rely on them as descriptors.

When people speak, they do not realize that what they are saying is not the truth. It is a representation of experience. It is not the experience itself.

The significance of this becomes obvious when I compare my grammar to that of the Ojibway and the Cree. Their languages have neither a division of time nor of gender. A Cree friend told me that it is very difficult to indicate the past or the future in her native language.

The Cree language is divided by what is animate and what is inanimate. A chair is inanimate while a dog is animate. But the language has a yet further subtlety when defining animation. The chair becomes animate when a human touches it. Thus, for example, a gun, labeled inanimate cannot accidentally be fired. For once a human touches it, it is animated. This distinction is embedded in the language. And, of course, by implication, a kind of responsibility is therefore also embedded in the language.

As I contemplated the Cree and Ojibway languages, I speculated on whether or not feminism could exist in a language without gender designations. Or how exactly one saw birth and death if there is no time designation. Describing a world without time and without gender has to be very different from the one I inhabit. We often hear of native leaders speaking of ancestors. I also speak of ancestors, but I automatically place ancestors in the past. But if my language does not have a way to designate the past, then when I speak of my ancestors, I am speaking of them in the present.

I think of the Oka crisis which occurred in response to the development of a golf course over burial grounds of ancestors. If I cannot describe my ancestors except in the present, such a thing would be unthinkable.

It is not that we cannot express ourselves in English in the present moment. It is just that we rarely do. When we do, it is usually through metaphor. Poets do it best. But it is not poetry that most people read every day. Rather most people read prose, deeply conditioned by time and space. Again, this is the language of the horizontal axis, the language of the mundane, time defined. The language of the vertical axis is timeless. It is the language of metaphor.

One of my favorite poets is Wallace Stevens. In his poem *Sunday Morning*, he describes the impending nightfall:

At evening, casual flocks of pigeons make
Ambiguous undulations as they sink,
Downward to darkness, on extended wings.

We read this and wonder, "What is he talking about? What is a casual flock? What are ambiguous undulations? Which way does darkness happen, anyhow? Whose wings?" Stevens makes us stop. He interrupts our patterns of thought about evening. He inflects another reality onto ours. He moves us to the vertical axis. It is beautiful.

The Church and Beauty

The Christian faith has always held beauty in high esteem. One need only spend time in Europe visiting cathedrals to experience how beauty was revered. It was certainly viewed as an important access point to spirit. Cathedrals are immense physical structures designed to bring humans into the experience of spirit. Ironically, the current inflection towards the mundane that we see in Western life was, in some ways, created out of an artificial split between the sacred and the profane that occurred in the early Christian church. While medieval sacred manuscripts were painstakingly made beautiful by illuminations, paintings depicting biblical events or elaborate patterns indicating the mystery of the spirit, they were also made in isolation from day-to-day life. Monks in monasteries separated from secular life dedicated their lives to the production of these beautiful texts. When the church held great power, it claimed the largest buildings in towns and villages, employing hundreds of workers to build them as well as artists to create sacred art, from sculptors to glass workers to composers. Because many of the villagers were employed by the church, and because community celebrations like marriages and christenings took place there, life was inflected with an awareness of spirit.

But the essential mysteries of the spirit were withheld from the vast majority of participants. By holding on to the secrets, religious leaders isolated themselves from their parishioners and ultimately assisted them to

put their attention on the visible rather than
the invisible. As populations grew, govern-
ments attempted to organize the societies.
Business began to outdistance the government
as employers and it became the prominent
inflection in life. Commerce is, of course, the
ultimate in the visible. And it is the ultimate
in the mundane. It is characterized by time
constraints and by measurements. This item
has to be produced in a certain amount of time
in order to be delivered to that customer on
schedule. Naturally, if people spend most of
their time engaged in mundane matters, they
begin to think this is life. When they make
that step they are choosing the mind/heart
axis as a ground for their experience. Then,
the body/spirit axis is often ignored. But, if
to be fully human means living a balanced life
between mind, heart, body and spirit, then
somehow we need to reclaim or relationship
to the North/South axis. How we might do
that is by consciously inflecting our lives with
beauty.

Living in Beauty

To show the difference between a life lived inflected with beauty and one without, I am going to relate a story that came from a friend of mine. He lives in the Yukon Territory, a vast and remote region of the Canadian Arctic.

"Kate, you won't believe this," he began, "but it really happened. I was driving along a highway just last week and I could see in the distance something that looked like a curtain. It looked like we were driving towards a curtain. I couldn't quite make it out but as we got closer I realized it was a curtain of snow. We were going to drive into a curtain of snow! It was amazing. I found myself getting more excited the closer we got to it until we were in it. We were in a curtain of snow! And, do you know that when we were in it I could see every single snowflake as a separate thing? Each one looked like a diamond. We were driving in diamonds! It was beautiful."

As he told me this story, he became increasingly animated and I found myself feeling almost as joyful listening to it as he was in the telling of it.

Then he said something else. "You know," he continued, "my friend, driving with me in the same car at the same time didn't see it. She said, 'I don't want to see any more snow.' She didn't see the curtain and she didn't see the diamonds."

On the one hand, you have a man who is completely immersed in the experience of "a curtain of snow". On the other hand, you have a person who cannot see the curtain for the snow. That is the point. When one is having an experience of beauty, one is 'in' the experience. It is an experience of depth.

Let's look more carefully at the experience. What was happening to my friend? First, he was fully in the present. He was experiencing nothing outside of the "curtain". Second, he was fully alert. Third, there was no consciousness of time. Fourth, there was no judgment taking place. And finally, he had entered a state of awe and wonder. My friend had connected with his spirit. His friend had connected with her mind.

His friend took all her past experience and feelings about snow and applied them to what she was seeing. Her judgments and evaluations determined what she would perceive. She was coming from the past rather than the present. Being in the moment was not a possibility for her because she had mentally conditioned the experience. Thus she had no access to spirit.

You see, entering into beauty is an action,

a doing. We have to choose it to go there. We have to be fully awake to receive it. It is always a present experience. Equally, living in the mind is also a choice. What is interesting about these choices is that most of the time we are unconscious about them. Most of the time, we do not realize we are choosing to experience what we experience.

Somehow we have come to believe that what we experience is happening to us, as if an outside force made us experience life. To me this is giving away our personal power to randomness. Life is a choice, not an accident. Living in beauty is a choice and a natural one at that.

Think of your early childhood, before you were seven years old, before school descended on you. Your life was big and bold and beautiful. That was your natural state. If you had a chair and a blanket you could create a fort. And it *was* a fort to you. That kind of imagination comes when life is beautiful. So does magic. I was walking along a seawall

on the way to my studio. A friend had been
visiting me for the past week. One of our
favorite things to do is to walk. So we walked
along the seawall, in forests, on city streets.
We walked and walked and talked and talked
and sometimes just walked in silence. One
of the things about walking with my friend
is that for some reason I don't understand, we
always walk shoulder-to-shoulder. No part
of our bodies touch except our shoulders. I
don't know why this happens but it always
does. In any case, as I was walking alone the
day after his departure I was lamenting the
fact that there was no shoulder beside me. I
missed it being there. In my mind I could
imagine it there. But it wasn't. So, I was on
the edge of sadness. Suddenly, out of nowhere,
a big, beautiful, white Russian Wolfhound
appeared at my side and for some fifty yards
it walked right next to me. We walked hip-
to-hip. I could feel this beautiful creature
right up and down my body. It was glorious.
Then, just as suddenly, it turned away and left

me. By that time, I was enraptured by the experience and had completely forgotten the missing shoulder.

It is, of course, amazing that that animal should choose to walk beside me, touching me, just at that moment. And although that is important, what is really important is that I paid attention. I let the experience of the dog into my awareness and received the beauty of the moment. I could have reacted in a variety of ways, from ignoring it, to shooing it away to stopping to look for its master. I could have continued to wallow in my self-pity but I didn't. I had been given a gift of beauty and I welcomed it. This is always the case with beauty. We have to let it in. And it will come to us.

Location of Beauty

Where do we find beauty? We find it everywhere. There is the potential to find beauty in every single experience we have in life, in every physical location and in every interpersonal communication. It is not so much whether or not beauty is present. It is whether or not we allow it up into our consciousness.

It's interesting that people of advanced consciousness are able to see beauty in all forms. To them, not only is all of life sacred, but all form is beauty.

The Natural World 🦋

The first and most obvious place to look for beauty is in the world around us, particularly the natural world. Here is where we see glorious sunsets, rainbows, diamonds on the sea, flowers that take our breath away, the elegance of wild creatures and trees ten stories high.

I am very lucky to live in Vancouver, one of the most beautiful cities in the world. It is a tranquil and seductive city where mountains and ocean meet. In this city, it is completely acceptable to leave work early on a sunny day so that you can walk on the beach. When I first moved here, I found myself taking the long way everywhere. I would walk along the beach even if I was on my way to the bank. And I would get to the bank just before closing and say, "Is it really 4:30? Where did the afternoon go? Well, I just had to take a detour to the beach on my way here." The teller would look at me, smile and with a knowing look say, "Why, of course, you *had* to do that." And she was not being facetious.

Vancouver is a magical, enchanting city. One day, I looked out my living room window and noticed a bald eagle sitting atop a very old, very tall fir tree. I watched it for some time, marveling that I was in the middle of a large city and an eagle was my neighbor. While I was watching, it took flight, dropping down, flying right past my third-floor window. If the window had been open, I could have reached out and touched it. My mouth dropped open. All I could say was "Oh!" On another occasion, I was wandering along the beach when a coyote stepped out onto the beach and surveyed the territory. It was absolutely still, simply looking. I stopped and watched. Then it turned and disappeared. What is there to say but *wow*?

The mountains stand as sentinels over the city. It is impossible to be lost in Vancouver because as soon as you see the mountains you know where North is. There is nothing quite like turning onto a North/South street and seeing the mountains pop up in front of you. Even if you are having a very busy day, have appointments to keep and problems to solve, just for a moment you find yourself forgetting them as you look up and breathe in, breathe out.

The other beauty of this city is the light. I am not a painter so I don't really know what it is, but there are days when the light is luminous. Or perhaps it is the shadow. I am not sure which. For example, as the fall equinox approaches, the light hits the city at an angle that seems to put everything into high relief. On these beautiful warm, sunny days — the sky a clear blue, a very light breeze whispering against the skin — every detail of the landscape is available to be seen. Many people comment on it. And many have said, "It's why I live here."

One of the beauties of living in Canada is the proximity to the wilderness, of untouched nature. I grew up in a small Northern Ontario town. My town was situated around a freshwater lake, one of the many scattered through the North. It was also directly in the middle of a forest. Its roads and sidewalks and streetlights were surrounded by this dense forest. I recall walking with my father from my home into the forest about two blocks away. Because my father grew up in my town, he also knew the forest surrounding it. We were looking to find our family a Christmas tree and I, age five at the time, was 'helping' him. Father carried nothing but an axe as we moved into the forest. I remember him telling me not to walk on what looked like a small hill because that might be where a bear was hibernating. He delivered that instruction as a fact and I did not feel in the least that I was in any danger. In fact, I felt quite the opposite. I was safe. I was beside my father and among the trees. And we were immersed in silence. For there is nothing quite like the silence of a winter forest. The pianist Glenn Gould called it "an image of the North" that most Canadians carry in their consciousness. I believe him to be correct. The wilderness in our country is profoundly important to us. We can both visit its majesty in physical terms and through our imagination. Indeed, for many of us it is a saving grace, balancing our time-driven daily lives.

The capacity we have for visiting places of beauty and tranquility using memory and imagination is enormously healing to the spirit. It is the not paying attention that so annoyed our teachers in grade school. We often found ourselves daydreaming. Why? Because we were overwhelmed by the mundane. By the ever-continuing listing of facts that threw us into boredom. It is the same reason we daydream as adults while in long, often insufferable meetings. So instead of holding to the mundane, we enter the world of our imaginations. Now, if we have had profound experiences of beauty and silence in nature, we may find ourselves returning there. I recall standing on the edge of the Grand Canyon for the first time. Not a word was spoken. It is jaw-dropping, gob-smacking, magnificent. On the same trip, I climbed a butte near Monument Valley. The climb was a little nerve-wracking given that I have vertigo when I go up to the third step on a ladder, but on the top was a world I could never have imagined. There were caves in the sandstone and beautiful red arches under which I could stand and gaze out over the miles of desert around me. There was an alpine meadow with a variety of grasses and a beautiful creek making its way across it. There were goats munching on the grasses and there was the turquoise blue sky. And there was silence. The way I describe it to this day is that I felt I was standing in the hand of God. I could have quite happily remained there forever. And, of course, because I did go there, I can still access the experience because I climbed that rock and I stood there.

This is the thing about our experiences with nature. We have the opportunity to be in it, to engage fully, to be absolutely present, to experience depth. When we literally touch the earth as I did in Northern Arizona, we are making a spiritual experience physical and it does not leave us. We carry it with us forever — its beauty, its majesty, its silence. Anywhere, at any time, we can access the experience through memory and imagination. And indeed, we often do. It is the nature of the spirit to balance us when we are mired in the mundane. We may look up from our desks and see a shadow on the building beside us and suddenly we are transported to an experience we had twenty-five years before when we were climbing in some caves in Greece. We feel the coolness as we step out of the sun, hear the ocean as the surf crashes onto the adjacent beach and we find ourselves taking a deep long sigh.

A friend once told me a story about a coworker in her office. Apparently every day, the first thing this woman does when she comes into the office is to go to an internet site, find an image she likes and then print it and subsequently tack it up on her bulletin board. Each day, it is a new image. My guess is that she finds something beautiful, something that touches her spirit so that she can look up from her desk at any time during the day, see it and be nourished by it. The thing that is also interesting about this is that other people in the office are fascinated by this action and every day they find a reason to see what today's image is. Although they can't explain it, they know that something is going on. This is not a physical experience of whatever it is she has chosen, but it is a physical action with an intention to have the spirit nourished during her day of doing mundane things. She has learned to seek for and establish the conditions in which this beauty can be seen.

Nature is so generous, we need only step into her to receive her magnificence and to be fed by it. When I lived in Toronto, I had developed the habit of going for a walk each evening after supper. One of the highlights of that walk was a cardinal that would sit on the top of a particular tree and sing, every evening. It was truly wonderful to behold. One evening on one of these walks, I encountered a woman who had noticed I walked in the neighborhood each evening. She asked me about my walking and I told her that it began as a recommendation from my physiotherapist to help me heal a back injury and that I enjoyed it so much I just continued doing it. She responded by telling me a story about her summer vacation. She and her family vacationed at a lodge in Northern Ontario. Every evening, the whole family would take a walk together. They met a psychiatrist there who was also on vacation. He commented on their evening walk together. "You know," he said, "if every family did what you are doing each evening, I wouldn't have any work." Experiencing nature is a powerful antidote to the stresses of life.

The Exterior Public World

This is the world that we share together. It is

sidewalks and alleyways, parks and boulevards, bridges and bicycle paths. These are man-made and can be inflected with the beauty of art and nature. Here man's ingenuity and creativity make it possible to make utilitarian pathways beautiful. In Vancouver, this is done in a variety of ways. Most of the shoreline in the central part of the city has been allocated as public space. Walkways and bicycle paths meandering through parklands make the ocean accessible to everyone. The beaches are groomed daily and benches and sitting logs are available to everyone. One of the city's art galleries sponsors a public art program installing large sculptures intermittently along the various shorelines. Gardens have been planted and are regularly tended, sometimes by members of the neighborhood, sometimes by city workers. The result is that citizens find themselves called by the beauty around them and frequently take walks or rides or simply sit and watch a sunset. Interestingly, people do not bring radios and CD players to the beach. The expectation is silence.

Businesses, too, have become aware of the draw that beautiful public space has to people and so neighborhood business associations have been formed to create joint projects to beautify their exterior surroundings. Thus, lush baskets of flowers hang on walls and planters dot sidewalks and boulevards. Occasionally, sculptures decorate neighborhoods as well.

Bridges are decorated with banners created by local artists and, normally, these change according to the seasons. These works by artists along with the public art series provide public conversation. When one sculpture was erected in my neighborhood, people would stop and look at it. Some wanted to interpret it. "What is it?" they would say. Others simply admired. Nevertheless, it provided a focal point for community to occur.

Because I live in North America, I think in terms of enhanced nature and sculpture as public domain. Europe is quite another matter. Architecture is an integral part of the beauty of a city. Centuries old, the beauty of ancient craftsmanship surrounds one when walking through a European city. Cathedrals with sculpture carved into the edifices, city squares with cobbled streets and ancient sculpture, immense columns rising to announce entrances to buildings. Skyscrapers of glass and steel, while impressive, do not, on average, inspire in the same way as cornices and pillars, nor do they have the warmth of old stone. The important point is the external public domain of beauty is one which we choose to create. It is our call.

The Exterior Private World

This is the world we share with others, but only invited guests. These are the places where we put our personal mark, whether it is our office, our studio or our home. Many years ago, I walked the Canadian Open golf tournament by following one of my favorite players, Craig Stadler. I never understood until that day that the green is the golfer's office. As each golfer arrived at the green, he took possession of it. Each player inspected the green very carefully, bending over to remove debris, walking distances, seeing in ways I realized I didn't. I cannot explain it exactly, but I was aware that the professional golfers owned the greens. Although I am not a golfer, I have played a few rounds from time to time. Watching these men play made me realize that I knew nothing about playing this game. Not a thing. I felt honored to be allowed to witness their intense focus, their clarity and the depth to which they created a relationship with their environment. They were in the green. It was beautiful to see.

This is what our opportunity is in our homes and, if we are lucky, our workplaces. For example, I was once a little early for an appointment with my lawyer and spent some extra time sitting in the reception area. A man and a woman came in and sat down near me. I gathered that they were former partners in the firm as everyone who walked through recognized them and stopped to speak to them. Behind the receptionist's desk hung a large and interesting painting. The woman spoke to her partner and said, "I am sure that painting used to be in the boardroom. I got to know it well through those many long meetings we had there." The painting provided her with a place to go outside the mundane in the meetings. She may not remember the details of the meetings she attended, but she remembers the beauty of the art in the room.

Beauty is worth keeping. A good friend of mine lives in a beautiful, spacious home adjacent to a golf course. Her children have now moved away from home and there has been considerable discussion about whether or not they should sell their home and find a smaller place.

My girlfriend has always wanted to create an exotic garden in the backyard. Some time ago, she became ill and was unable to work. As a healing project for herself, she decided to design and implement the garden of her dreams. Her husband could not understand her enthusiasm but he was willing that she do what she wanted. So, she got quotes, hired contractors and created a stunning garden which is created on several levels and includes slate slabs as well as a water feature. The area is unrecognizable from what it once was. It is a refuge of beauty and silence, a source of delight and a place they can visit each day to fill their spirits. There is no longer any discussion about selling their home. They have decided to stay.

This is precisely what our homes can be for us if we are mindful and if we choose to inflect them with beauty. They can be refuges from the cares and concerns of working life. Making one's home beautiful is a popular notion at the moment, thanks to the many experts who design home makeovers on television and to the widespread availability of materials. The important thing is that the home you create speaks to you, nourishes you. This is where you come to be regenerated so what your home contains should be those things which inspire you and bring you back to your self.

I have a couple of friends who are artists. Their home is filled with objects, some that are natural such as pieces of wood or interesting rocks and some that are their own creations. Every available surface from tabletops to walls to window ledges have fascinating things on them. The walls of their home are painted in bright turquoises and reds and greens. They designed and built the house themselves and have a huge Douglas fir tree growing out of the middle of their deck. Instead of cutting it down, they built around it.

Another couple I know has created a series of circular pathways in their garden leading to a meditation pyramid. A few years ago, they visited Turkey and were so inspired by the architecture and design there that they have created one room in their home that feels like a home in Turkey. They even dismantled one of their bathrooms and created a steam bath for themselves.

A third couple were both born in Europe. Their home is baroque in style and color. It contains beautiful pieces of furniture, sculpted and textured. Fabrics are rich in deep burgundies and gold.

Each home is beautiful in its own way. Each speaks to the spirits of those who live there. None follows current fashion trends. Rather, they express the passions and tastes of the people who live in them. This is always our opportunity. Instead of viewing our homes as real estate investments we can view them both as expressions of our inner creativity and as opportunities to create safe havens for regeneration of our spirits. We can create our personal world which moves us to step out of the mundane.

Personal Physical Beauty

Physical Practice

There is considerable discussion today about staying fit and keeping the body in good health. Indeed, the fitness revolution over the past several decades has resulted in the creation of a new multi-billion dollar industry which includes alternative health practitioners, personal trainers, home fitness equipment, private gyms, fitness clothing lines, health food stores, vitamin stores and even "healthy heart" choices on restaurant menus. So, there is certainly awareness and even agreement that care of the body is important. The question is, why is it important?

If we return to the Medicine Wheel, we notice that the body is on the vertical axis along with the spirit. Remembering that this is the axis of joy and magic and beauty, we understand that the body is important. The spirit expresses itself through the physical and our personal spirits express themselves through our individual physical bodies. Care of the body, then, implies care of the spirit.

The relationship between body and spirit is well known in Eastern cultures. Practices such as yoga, tai chi and whirling all integrate body and spirit. In the West, this awareness has traditionally come through sport. There are many documentations of 'being in the zone'. But getting there occurs through repetitive actions, through practice. It is doing yoga every day that tones the body and makes it limber. It is a five-mile run every day that makes a long-distance runner. It is four to six hours in class every day that makes a dancer. It is through the practice of a physical discipline that the spirit expresses itself, that beauty appears. This is not beauty in the sense of the fashion runway. This is the revelation of the inner beauty of the spirit. We are part of a physical reality. In order to experience that reality, it is crucial that we ground ourselves in our physical bodies, that which allows us to be here.

Having the right workout clothes will not make a difference. Having the right trainer will not make a difference. Going to yoga class once a week will not make a difference. Repetition grounds the body. This is the most difficult of things. My current chosen physical practice is yoga. Six days of the week, the first thing I do after waking up is a 30 to 45-minute yoga routine. Although my body may look forward to it, day after day after day , my mind comes up with hundreds of distractions to entice me from starting my routine, shortening the exercises, saying it is okay if I don't stretch far enough and, of course, thinking about other things rather than what I am doing. It is amazing to me how ingenious my mind can be. I have been doing this practice for four years now and still, every day I can think of some reason not to do it. Every single time I begin my practice, I have to override my mind's better idea. And every day I complete my routine, I triumph. In other words, before I get dressed, have a shower, eat breakfast, indeed, before I am out of my bedroom, I have triumphed. What a way to start the day.

But it is even better than that. I am over sixty years old and am stronger, more alert and more physically capable than I was when I was forty. Dr. David R. Hawkins, a noted authority on human behavior, states, "We know clinically that alignment with beauty is associated with longevity and vigor — because beauty is a function of creativity, such longevity is common in all creative occupations."

Moreover, because I begin my day by

entering my body fully, my spirit is freed to fly. When we are children, just getting used to our bodies, we love to use them. We run rather than walk, we skip and dance and roll on the ground. We kick our feet and throw our hands up in the air. We climb and then jump. We are in our bodies and we fully experience the joy of that. As we grow older and the cares and responsibilities of the mundane world intrude into our lives, we find ourselves less engaged with our bodies. Instead we occupy ourselves with the cares of the world: our families, our work, our relationships, our responsibilities. All of these seem so important that they take precedence in our day-to-day lives. And all of these activities occur on the horizontal mind — heart axis. The repetitive behaviors we engage in are typically those which occur there.

Admittedly, some people have their regular squash game once a week or golf game or 10K run or they participate in some team sport. But, by and large, life revolves around the cares of the world. Unfortunately, too, we

have created a world which makes us depen-
dent on the automobile as our primary mode
of locomotion. Instead of a two-mile walk
to work each day, because we have imagined
time constraints, we drive. We deny ourselves
the opportunity to use our bodies and at the
same time experiencing nature is denied to us
by us. We make this decision and we are the
ones who can make different choices.

That does not mean that the choice is an
easy one, nor is it necessarily convenient. I
recently moved my studio to an island about
a mile from my home. It is an extraordinarily
beautiful walk to reach it as it is a seaside walk
with a five-minute ferry ride to the island.
And yet, for the first three months my studio
was located there, I drove every day. I had
very good reasons. There was this to carry and
it was too heavy for me over a mile's distance,
or I needed to pick up some bubble wrap for
shipping, or I had to pick up my mother to
take her to visit my father, or I had a hair-
cut scheduled or a lunch date. The list was

endless and always seemed real to me. More-over, I found myself increasingly testy about city traffic. When I got to work I was an-noyed, and when I arrived home I had some story to tell about some crazy driver.

One day I stopped, looked at what I was doing and chose to walk to work. I noticed that I loved the walk. I loved the sound of the water on the beach, the trees overhead, the sun in my face, the wind on my body, the smell of the air and the delight on the faces of the people I passed on the way. I was in wonderful humor when I arrived there, feel-ing invigorated and energized. Now, I find myself annoyed when I have to drive and make sure I arrange my errands for the studio on one day of the week so that I don't ever have to drive there more than once a week. Admittedly, approximately one half-hour has been added to my day, but what a return I am getting on that time investment. Now I frame my day of work (East/West axis) with the physical experience of using my body in nature (North/South axis).

It seems to me that modern life has two prevailing currencies which drive it: time and money. Notice that both currencies are landmarks of the East/West axis, the mundane world. What I am suggesting here is that we choose to add a third currency. We choose to add a currency that adheres to the North/South axis and that is the currency of the spirit, the currency of joy and beauty. This can occur in a variety of ways but one of the simplest and most accessible, and certainly the cheapest, is to simply use our bodies in ways that delight us and bring joy to us. Walking in nature is one of those very simple things that can help to balance the cares of our lives. Perhaps, if one has chosen to live in the suburbs and must commute to work, she can park her car a mile from her office (where parking is likely to be cheaper) and then walk the rest of the way to the office. Because most of us have already established a pattern of going to work, adding a pattern of physical

engagement that occurs around our current pattern may be the easiest thing to do.

Adornment

For the first six years of my life, I lived in a small house with my family. This house was part of my grandparents' property and was immediately behind their home. Consequently, my grandparents and their friends were part of my extended family in those early years. In particular, my grandmother (whom I called Nanny) and her two best friends, Mrs. Corres and Mrs. Dee, were the important elders in my world. Mrs. Corres and Mrs. Dee lived directly across the street from my grandmother. Thus, one or the other of these women would watch over me from their front porches whenever I played in the front yard or on the street. Their presence is deeply etched in my memory.

To my young eyes, grandmothers were large women. They were tall and wide. They wore corsets and stockings and square shoes with heels and dresses, housedresses if at home (often with a full length apron over them) and suits, gloves and hats if they were going out. I can remember sitting at the bottom of the stairs at my grandmother's house, watching her come down the stairs dressed to go to one of her Eastern Star meetings. She wore a beautifully tailored navy blue wool suit (which she had made), a gorgeous sparkly large brooch on her lapel, a string of pearls around her neck and trailing over her left shoulder was a mink stole. But this wasn't just any mink stole, this one had the heads and feet of the animals as part of it. I thought she was the most exotic and wonderful woman I had ever seen. I was lucky enough to inherit that mink stole and as I sit here, it is mounted on a sculpture beside me.

These three women provided me with the imprint of what a woman is. My brother was very ill and my mother was preoccupied with him (my mother had been instructed not to allow him to cry for the first two years of his life) and so the grandmothers stepped in where I was concerned. All were elegant women. All were kind and all were busy. They sewed, knit, crocheted and baked. Indeed, my mother tells me that I had 52 dresses by the time I was two years old. Since these women made their own clothes, they simply made dresses for me as well with the extra fabric. And they always dressed. It didn't matter if they were washing the kitchen floor, they did so wearing a dress and stockings and shoes. If we went on a picnic, they were dressed. If they walked to the post office, they were dressed. If they accompanied me to the park, they were dressed. They always wore jewelry (earrings at the very least). They had their hair done once a week. And they smelled wonderful. These were big-breasted, blowsy ,enormous women and they were fabulous.

There was backbone to these women. They were certain of their place in the world and confident of their value. Consequently, they looked after themselves. That is not to say that they didn't look after others. My own experience is a testament to their generosity. But their days began, first, with a practice of caring for themselves, of pampering themselves with powders and creams, of dressing carefully and well, of adorning themselves with appropriate jewelry and cosmetics. And as well as they were dressed in the mornings, if, for example, they were to attend an afternoon meeting, before that they dressed again appropriately prior to going out. There was a consciousness about how they presented themselves to the world. Their outer appearance was a statement that represented themselves and their families. But, further than that, they changed their clothes in order to step out of the mundane, daily routine. One of the ways of shifting from the mundane to the beautiful is to simply change our clothes. We are then making a conscious inflection towards beauty.

In some respects, I wonder if the changing of clothes to suit the occasion reflects the attainment of a certain status, a state of 'eligibility'. In traditional mystic teachings, students move up to become Masters when they are eligible. Eligibility is a field of energy that includes knowledge and right action. I sometimes wonder if, in our quest for comfort, we are giving up the power to experience fully. Being eligible is not comfortable. It is a state of alertness. And alertness is needed if we want to experience beauty. I was once in a shop and overheard women talking about how soft and comfortable a line of clothing was. I looked over to see what they were talking about and saw some soft fabrics and shapeless designs. I am not saying that soft fabrics aren't wonderful. Rather, I am wondering what this quest for comfort concerns. The experience of beauty is not a passive one. It requires engagement and participation. It requires alertness and attentiveness. It does not come to us accidentally. It comes to us when we are eligible to receive it. It comes to us because we make it so.

When I think of elegantly adorned men and women, I must admit that I think of Fred Astaire and Ginger Rogers. In their movies, they always dressed appropriately for the occasion. And there were lots of occasions. To some degree, the world of my grandmothers was similar. When I think of the Astaire movies, one word comes to mind: grace. Not just in movement, but also in style. Manners, language, interior design, fashion and, of course, dance.

I miss the grace I witnessed in my grandmother's home and those of her friends. Whether or not we will ever retrieve that remains to be seen, for the roles women play in life are much more complex than those my grandmother played.

A few months after I first began selling my jewelry, I went to the opera. I dressed carefully for my evening out, mindful of the tradition of the theatre. I was delighted to be going as I was to see a performance of *La Bohème*, one of my favorites. I decided that during the intermission I would, as a bit of market research, notice what jewelry women were wearing. In particular, I would look at pendants and necklaces largely because these are my favorites to make. I walked around all three of the lobbies noticing what women were wearing. I was horrified to see only two necklaces. Women simply were not wearing jewelry. In fact, many were not dressed up at all. From the point of view of my business, this was a disaster. How was I going to make a living at jewelry if no one was wearing it? But the larger question was: do women not want to adorn themselves any more? Do they not want to be beautiful?

My guess about why this is happening is the current poverty of time. Women are raising families as well as pursuing careers. Taking time to change before attending the theatre is simply not on their radar screens. Comfort and effortlessness supercede representation of the self. Time is the dominant inflection in life rather than spirit. Certainly the act of

going to the opera is an action which is intended to move one out of everyday experience into wonder for, if nothing else, opera is certainly spectacle. So, it is not that women do not understand the importance of beauty. Rather, it seems, they do not consider adornment to be essential in their own personal experience and representation of it.

Many years ago I was reading a book in which a powerful sorceress played a significant role. This woman was very old and yet she had lustrous black hair and an ageless, beautiful face. She wore bright, beautiful clothing which contained intricately woven patterns. Another character asked her if she was using a disguise so that she could look so young and beautiful. She did not answer him directly. But I have never forgotten her words. They went something like this: "Beauty is one of woman's natural powers." I had never really thought of beauty as a power and yet, when I think of how beauty stops the mind, I cannot dispute her words.

To give up our beauty in favor of comfort is to give away our power. To be able to use our natural power, we must bring it into consciousness. This, of course, means putting our attention on it and doing something about it. It means taking care of hair, nails, cosmetics, wardrobe and jewelry. It means getting to know what looks best on us regardless of fashion. For example, one year brown may be the fashionable color. Well, that is all fine and good but I cannot wear brown. It turns my skin yellow. So that year I will not follow the trend. I refuse to give away my power to the vagaries of an industry. My power is mine to wield.

A few years ago my son, then a budding musician, realized that he would not be respected by club owners if he did not dress seriously. So he stopped wearing blue jeans and t-shirts and started wearing dress pants and smart sweaters. Suddenly he was booking gigs. Adornment matters.

Interpersonal Beauty

The only moment is now. That is what beauty does. It takes us to now. I once had a teacher who explained to me how people think they are 'in love'. On the Medicine Wheel, the mind and heart are on opposite ends of the horizontal axis. The body and spirit are on opposite ends of the vertical axis. In traditional teaching, the male is on the mind end of the horizontal axis and the female on the heart end. However, they meet in the South in the body. They have a profound physical experience through sex that shoots up the vertical axis to the spirit. Then they think, "This is love. I am in love." They proceed to marry and very quickly live their lives on the horizontal axis: who is going to take out the garbage? Why don't you understand how I feel? Do you have to sleep in front of the TV? They begin to move away from the profound experience that they once had. Then patterns are created and they live their lives through their patterns and they may even have a pattern called 'we fell in love when we met in Paris'. Once they live their lives through patterns, they lose spontaneity and openness and joy.

When sexual experiences are powerful, it is because both people are completely immersed in the experience. They let go of controls and patterns and enter the physical experience deeply and in the present. Always, always, this will move one to an experience of spirit, of the underpinnings of life and love. The problem, then, is how to keep that depth. The answer, of course, is that one must let it go. And then one gets to create another experience. They meet again and again in the present.

How, then, does one find beauty in the relationship once again? Is it possible? My friend tells me of an experience he had in South Africa. He was, at the time, studying with a couple who were Zen teachers. They were husband and wife. He recalls that theirs was the most beautiful marriage he has ever witnessed. He asked the woman how they did it, how did they have such a beautiful relationship? Her response was, "We treat every moment that we have together as if it is the only one we will ever have." That is, Now is all there is.

If, when we meet another, we can let go of both our history with that person and our expectations of him (both constructs of the mind, catalogued in our memories), we have the opportunity to create a new moment in time. It is here that joy resides. It is here that we can find beauty.

If we observe young children, this is exactly how they behave. I can remember very clearly being present when my three-year-old son woke up. His large, long-lashed blue eyes opened. He sat up, looked around and seemed to say, "Wow! What is going to happen today?" Every day was an adventure. Eating breakfast was an adventure. Walking to nursery school was an adventure. Meeting a stray dog on the street was an adventure. I recall a moment when we were returning home from nursery school. There was a large sheepdog that lived with a family on the corner. My son and I were walking by their yard when Major (the dog) came rushing over to the hedge barking loudly. My son looked up at me and said in his characteristically loud, ringing voice, "My, Major is chatty today, isn't he?" I burst into laughter as did my neighbors who were sitting in their back garden with the dog. There was no fear in my son's response, only joy that his friend, the dog (much bigger than the little boy) was excited and talking.

The opportunity to be present in the moment is always there for us if we can let go of the patterns that we cling to when we communicate. One of the familiar and comfortable social lubricants is the phrase, "How are you?" Normally, one answers, "Fine, thank you. How are you?" Largely, it has no meaning at all. Lately, I have started a campaign to respond to the question using unexpected beautiful language. If I am feeling terrific, I might say, "Incandescently glorious, thank you." Or if I am grumpy, I might say, "Moribund and taciturn, thanks." It is absolutely wonderful to see what happens when you say something like that. The pattern has been interrupted and people are thrown back into the moment. Jaws drop and often laughter ensues. And why not experience joy rather than boredom?

That's the thing about relationships and the beauty in them. We choose them. We create them. It is not, of course, a simple matter to have a beautiful relationship. It is, however, a worthy one. The most difficult thing of all is to simply accept a communication as it comes to us without judgment. Mostly, we jump ahead while the other is speaking, anticipating our response before the other has even completed his statement. It is a matter of honoring the other that is required.

About two weeks ago, I had lunch with a good friend. For some reason, on that day, we somehow managed to speak and simply receive each other's offerings. I am not sure why it happened but it was a truly beautiful experience. He would say something, sometimes at length, and I would listen carefully to what he had to say but instead of responding to some detail, I would simply nod or smile. He did the same to me. It was rather like dancing. Often we talked about completely different things, but depending on who was speaking, the one would follow the other to wherever he was going. For some two hours, we managed not to judge what the other was saying. The result was a magical, mysterious dance of beauty. We have the choice to let either the mind or the spirit run our communications.

One of the mind's favorite strategies to managing conversation and experience is to think attack ideas. This can be seen most clearly when one is driving. "What does that jerk think he is doing?" we might ask ourselves. In that moment, we have uttered an attack thought. Of all the things the mind does to sabotage our experience of beauty, attack thoughts and statements are the most damaging. For when we think them or use them, we create an environment of fear around us and ultimately we attack ourselves, for we create anxiety in ourselves. Of all the things we can do to relearn the experience of beauty, derailing attack thoughts may very well be the most powerful. One of the best places to practice this is while driving. So many things happen on the road when one is driving that frequently result in our thinking attack thoughts towards others that this is the perfect place to observe our attack patterns and then interrupt them. I have been doing this for some time now and now it is very interesting for me to drive with others, for inevitably someone will express an attack thought towards another driver. Sometimes I make a healing comment to counter the attack, and sometimes I just receive it and watch carefully what my mind is doing. The experience of driving is much more relaxed for me now because my mind is under my control (at least where other drivers are concerned). The challenge is to carry that into everyday life.

Beauty, Men and Women

In the course of writing this book, something rather unexpected has come up. I had right from the outset assumed that my readership would be women. And this may be true, but it is *not* true that men are not interested in beauty. On every occasion that I have spoken to a man about this project, every single man has responded with something like "Beauty, eh? Let me tell you about an experience of beauty I had." These stories that the men tell me are stunningly beautiful. Let me give you a short example. I was once having coffee with a friend and we got talking about my book. He actually shared two very beautiful stories. This is one of them.

"I was visiting my parents and we were reminiscing. I said to them that I bet they had lots of stories to tell about us kids. Now, my father was a very quiet man. He rarely spoke, though he was always kind to us. He said to me, 'What I remember about you is what happened when you were brought home from the hospital after having surgery when you were three months old. We put you down on the bed. You were smiling and kicking your feet. I leaned over you and brought my face close to yours. You reached up with your little hand and touched my face. It was the first time in my life that I recognized that love could come through touch.' Kate, I looked at my father after he told me this and realized we both had tears in our eyes."

What I have come to learn is that men experience beauty deeply and frequently. But they rarely talk about it. I asked my 29-year-old son about this. He said a couple of things that were rather provocative. First, he commented that he had been with three other men, sitting on a beach watching the sunset. He told me that "I know that every one of us got how beautiful it was. No one spoke. We just watched the sunset. And not one of us commented on it." I asked my son why he thinks that is. He says he doesn't know for sure but that it just isn't done among men.

"You know," he said, "that is the thing that I think men look for in women. We look to them to open up the conversation about beauty. And you know what else? It is almost impossible right now to find a woman who will make that opening for us."

Just today, I had an interesting conversation with a woman who owns a clothing store. We were talking about beauty and she told me this story: "You know, Kate, I learned about beauty from my father. When I was very young, I remember on many occasions being with him. He would encounter something beautiful and he would stop whatever we were doing and look. He would stop talking and he would stop doing. He wouldn't say a word, would be completely silent. I was fascinated by this and eventually realized that he always stopped whenever he saw something beautiful. So, gradually, I learned to do the same thing." It was her father, not her mother, who taught her about beauty.

After this woman told me this story, her assistant shared the following. "You know, when my fiancé and I first started dating, I would point out this or that that I found to be beautiful. I notice that now he points things out to me." Clearly, what she has done is provide an opening for her fiancé to find and even comment on beauty. I wonder if this isn't the opportunity for all women in their relationships with men. And I wonder if we shouldn't do something about it. It strikes me that relationships could be improved simply by couples sharing experiences of beauty, for when they do so, they have the opportunity to touch spirit, the very thing that probably brought them together in the first place.

Reclaiming Beauty

We all need to "use beautiful words and offer
beautiful music, and create beauty in the
environment."

— *Masaru Emoto*

The opportunity, then, is to reclaim beauty
as an integral and essential part of our lives.
For reclamation to occur, however, beauty is
going to require currency in our lives. If we
accept that beauty enriches the spirit and
stills the mind and further, we accept that this

has value, we will find a place to both receive and create beauty.

Receiving Beauty

When I was a child attending family gatherings at my grandmother's, we ate at a large table in the dining room. We all dressed in our Sunday best. The china was Booth's Real Old Willow and the crystal was Waterford. My grandmother always made an event of these gatherings. My family would arrive mid-morning and my grandmother would sweep me into the kitchen where she would have made donuts for me. I was allowed to have two if I wanted. Then we would join my grandfather in the living room and he would regale us with one story after another. My grandfather was Scottish by birth and was a gifted singer and storyteller.

He was a policeman, the kind of policeman who, when he found a boy making trouble, would, instead of putting him in jail, take him home to his parents. When he died, the church was overflowing into the street with people.

Over 100 policemen marched in formation in full dress uniform from the church, accompanying the coffin the three miles to the cemetery. My grandfather was not killed in the line of duty. He died of natural causes in old age.

I remember arriving at my grandparents' home very early one Christmas morning. Grandfather came into the house in uniform. He had worked the graveyard shift. I was very excited about this.

"Did you see Santa Claus?" I asked.

"Well," he said as he got down on his knee beside me. "At about two o'clock in the morning, I parked the cruiser in the empty lot beside Poudrette's (my favorite variety store). I heard some noise and looked up into the sky and, smooth as you can imagine, a sleigh and eight reindeer swooped over me, circled around and landed right beside the car."

No doubt my eyes must have been as

wide as saucers.

"The sleigh was overflowing with gifts and the reindeer shook their coats and stamped the snow making the bells on their harnesses ring out. A very big man, with a long snowy beard, dressed all in red climbed out of the sleigh and walked towards the car. I opened the door and stood beside him. You know, Kate, he was this much taller than me."

Grandfather raised his arm and reached way above his head. I was transfixed.

"I thought maybe he would like a cigar and so I offered him one of mine. We lit them and then stood side-by-side watching the smoke as it rose up into the sky. We didn't talk much, just enjoyed our cigars. Now don't you tell Grandma this. She doesn't like me smoking cigars and she will be annoyed that I gave Santa one."

I nodded my head. I was sure that if Santa smoked a cigar with my grandfather, it was probably O.K.

"Did you tell him I wanted a doll with

hair, Grandfather?"

"No, Kate, I did not do that. Santa has a big job to do and I don't think I should tell him how to do his job. What do you think?"

"Oh," I said. "I am sure you are right, Grandfather. I am not the only little girl in the world."

"No," he said, pulling me towards him and wrapping his arms around me. I could feel the brass buttons of his uniform against my cheek. "But you are my special girl, aren't you?"

The image of Grandfather smoking a cigar with Santa Claus on Christmas morning remains with me to this day.

When we sat down for Christmas dinner, all food would be in bowls and on platters sitting on the table. Grandmother would have removed her apron. I usually sat near her and my Grandfather sat what seemed like miles away at the other end of the table. He would look at each of us and then say in his Scottish brogue:

"Some have meat and canna eat,

Some dinnae have meat and want it.
But we have meat and we can eat,
So praise the Lord, we thank it."

For just a moment after this, silence would descend. Then grandfather would pick up the platter of turkey and the feast would begin.

I realize now that these family meals were infused with love and gratitude — love among the family and gratitude for the bounty we were receiving. This environment of love and gratitude was a gift of enormous power. It was the ground of being upon which I stood as a young child. And it made it possible for me to receive all of the magic around me, to fully experience joy and wonder. It is a similar ground that one might want to create in order to be open to receive beauty.

Masura Emoto, the Japanese researcher who is investigating the crystalline structure of water and its relationship to language and thought, was once asked, "Have you come across a particular word or phrase in your research that you have found to be most helpful in cleaning up the natural waters of the world?"

"Yes," he replied. "There is a special combination that seems to be perfect for this, which is *love* plus the combination of thanks and appreciation reflected in the English word *gratitude*. Just one of these is not enough. Love needs to be based in gratitude, and gratitude needs to be based in love . . . the Japanese word for gratitude is *kan-sha*, consisting of two characters: *kan*, which means feeling, and *sha*, apology. It's coming from a reverential space, taking a step or two back."

In other words, in order to receive in gratitude, one must pause, step out of the ordinary, make room for beauty to enter. This is a profound change in behavior for most of us. Most of our days are immersed in matters of the mundane. And most of these matters feel incredibly important: events at work, events at home, events in the world, even personal emotional events. To receive beauty,

one must step out of these daily cares and choose to experience it. It is amazing how rarely we do that.

For ten years, my husband and I were art collectors. Our favorite thing to do on weekends and vacations was to visit art galleries and, if we were lucky, find a piece to buy and add to our collection. The result was that our walls were covered with magnificent pieces of art. For the first week or two after adding a piece to our collection, we would be enraptured by it. As time went by, we stopped noticing and it became background. Then we would buy another piece and rearrange the collection, moving pieces to different walls in order to accommodate the new piece. The whole collection was new again and we would reawaken to its beauty. It seemed that we needed to add to the collection in order to receive its beauty. This is the power that the mundane had over us. We moved it to the forefront in importance and let go of the things which nourished our spirits.

So, the purpose of the art collection seemed to become adding to it rather than being with it. That is, we needed more of it to get it rather than being grateful for what we had and allowing it to work its magic on us.

When we separated, I moved to a new location taking with me only a few favorite pieces. I set up my house following a couple of principles. One was to follow the Feng Shui practice of not having things in my home that were broken or cracked and not having anything I did not love. The second was to create little pictures, putting together things which enhanced each other so that when placed together they became a unity. Interestingly, when I did that, I realized that I had carried with me my whole life. For each item is connected to some important doing or being in my life. Though I did not choose to bring the items for that reason, it turns out that I did have a purpose in choosing them. What is also interesting is that there turned out to be a place for each valued item I brought and when placed together with care, they are all beautiful.

Now, however, instead of setting them aside and focusing on the mundane matters of my life, I choose to consciously acknowledge them. Every day, first thing in the morning, I take ten minutes, sitting in silence and paying attention to the beauty in my home. I silently express my gratitude for that beauty and for the part it plays in my life. It nourishes me and inspires me. It is the beginning of my day and the ground from which I take action in my life. Interestingly, I have noticed that over the time I have been doing this, the beauty around me is more available to my awareness than it used to be. I do not take it for granted. Many times during my day I find myself taking it in, receiving it with joy and wonder. And I repeatedly think how lucky I am.

This may seem trivial and I suppose, from the perspective of the mundane, it is even irrelevant. However, I am beginning to think that it is far more important than we realize. One year, there was a water crisis in Vancouver. That particular November, we had three times the normal rainfall in our city. As a result, there were mudslides on the surrounding mountains and the water reservoirs for the city were affected. The tap water for the city was full of silt and was undrinkable. We were advised to either drink bottled water or boil our tap water before drinking it. This caused considerable upset among the city's population and affected the restaurant business. Mind you, the bottled water business flourished.

In any case, I had to boil my water before I drank it. In my day-to-day life, this could certainly be an annoyance. Indeed, when speaking with the cashier at my local supermarket, she told me that people had been terribly grumpy over the past week. I, on the other hand, experienced it as a minor blip in my day-to-day life and, in some respects, as a gift. Mindful of Mr. Emoto's work with water crystals, I realized that being grateful for the water, I would affect the crystalline structure of the water and so I decided to, as often as I could remember, be grateful for the water before I drank it. I would, bless the water as my grandfather did our family meals when I was a child. Instead of finding myself annoyed, I enjoyed taking the time to care for and appreciate the water I was lucky enough to have. Somehow, this process I was entering into felt beautiful to me and the water I drank a great gift.

When we are grateful, it is amazing what becomes beautiful. Just as the water cleared and we were allowed to drink it again, we had a huge snowfall in the city. It had been sixteen years since such a snowfall descended on the city that early in the season. It was shocking to all of us. And, oh, so beautiful. Because we live in an area which is essentially a rainforest, we have a profusion of very tall trees in our city. Thus the network of branches above us appeared as yards and yards of white lace. It lasted for three days. On the second day, I made it to my studio, which is on the second floor overlooking a marina. I entered and stopped, transfixed by the beauty around me. The whole of the marina was covered in snow: the masts of the sailboats, their decks, the heavy equipment used to lift the boats out of the water. Against a blue sky and blue water were mysterious shapes and shadows, a cool beauty. When such a natural event occurs, we have the opportunity to either resist it or move with it. If we can allow ourselves to receive it, magic happens and we do not notice that it is hard.

When my eldest son was six years old, we lived in a part of the country that sometimes received very heavy snowfalls. Many years, I had to shovel the driveway almost daily from the beginning of December to the middle of March. Once, the snowbanks in my driveway were well over my head and I realized that if it snowed again, I would not be able to lift the shovel high enough. Fortunately, it did not snow again that season. In any case, that winter we built a skating rink in our backyard. And the winter flew by. We were in it every single day, laughing and playing and, I might add, flooding the rink at midnight. It is one of the few winters I can remember when I didn't want the spring thaw to arrive. For the thaw, when it came, brought the end to our playground and an end to the enormous joy we had in being engaged with nature.

Receiving the beauty of nature is one thing. Receiving beauty which we create is quite another. My daughter-in-law has a friend who is a passionate knitter. Lisa reads the knitting blogs, develops and tries complex patterns, belongs to a knitting group and makes beautiful things. I was commenting to her one day how much her family must love to receive Christmas presents from her. "No," she said, "I don't ever knit for my family. They say 'oh, it's handmade' and they throw it away." This inability to receive a gift of beauty and love is the East/West axis at work, the mundane mind judging and evaluating.

There has been a decision made that things made by hand are not good and things made by machine are. That standardization is good and uniqueness is not. This is a rejection not of Lisa's offering but rather, a rejection by the receiver of life on the North/South axis, out of spirit.

In order to receive beauty, one chooses to let spirit inflect the response. Remembering Mr. Emoto's words, one receives from a "reverential space" taking "a step or two back." One must step back from the mundane and step into spirit. Interestingly, if Lisa had been a child offering knitting to her family, it is likely that her offering would have been received and even treasured. For even the most hardened adult generally reacts to the lightness of spirit that children bring. There is a kind of permission that adults give themselves when encountering children. It is not that adults don't know how to step into spirit. It is simply that their patterns of behavior among each other do not include

the "stepping back" required. The important thing to understand here is that this is a choice that they have made. It is not 'the truth.' Manufactured goods are not intrinsically better than handcrafted ones. It is just that manufactured goods can reach the mass market while handcrafted goods cannot. But, if one has inflected one's life with 'things' and the acquiring of them as a primary value, then one is choosing to live on the East/West axis rather than on the North/South. It is not the 'thing' which has value, but the accumulation of things.

Creating Beauty

Many years ago, I attended the Canadian National Exhibition. As in many communities across the country, every autumn a fall fair is held. The 'Ex' as we called it, is the biggest fall fair in the country. It is so big, it has permanent buildings on the grounds. These are huge cavernous affairs each devoted to one thing. There is a food building, an automotive building, a hobby building and many others. It was the hobby building which captured my imagination. It is an enormous structure, a huge convention-like space. In it, people exhibit their hobbies. As I walked through the many aisles, I became more and more excited. I could not believe what people do in their spare time. There were wooden toys, ships in bottles, model trains, knitted sweaters, popsicle stick buildings, model cars, jewelry made out of any number of materials, quilts, dolls, model cars and pewter figures. There were aisles and aisles of handcrafted things about which each vendor was passionate and enthusiastic. It was truly wondrous to behold. "This," I thought to myself, "is how truly creative people are." I was inspired and thrilled. It was like peeking into the secret lives of all these wonderful people. But what really struck me was their joy as they explained what they did and why they did it. To each and every exhibitor, what he or she created was beautiful. These people were exhibiting their treasures. But these treasures are not collected — they are created. I was enchanted.

A cynical person might find their passions hokey or childish: "I mean, really, grown men playing with toy trains." Or one might say, in a superior way, "Well, if you work on an assembly line all day, you would have to do something or you would go crazy." My response to that is "Yes and Yes and Yes!" That is exactly what is happening and how wonderful. Repetitive mind-numbing work (the East/West axis) demands some kind of relief for the spirit.

My father was a senior officer who directed investigations. Because of his senior position, he was required to be at the scene of every untimely death in his area. Recently, he became ill and my mother asked me to destroy his police files. They were voluminous and quite terrible. There were photographs in his files that no one should ever have to see. But he saw these events in real life. He never talked about his work. Never. Instead, he would come home, have dinner with us and go down to his workshop where he would begin hammering and sawing, creating some object of furniture. I now realize that this was what he did to balance out the terrible attacks on his spirit that he must have encountered again and again in his work. He had to create, for so much of his work brought him into contact with pain and destruction.

My father was also active in the Boy Scouts. He was, for many years, a scoutmaster and eventually a scout commissioner. Now I realize that his work brought him into contact with troubled young people and he was determined to do something to counter that. I do know, from stories my parents have told me, that more than one young man credits my father for saving him from trouble.

Creating beauty does not mean, necessarily, creating great works of art. It means becoming engaged in a process which interrupts the patterned experiences we encounter when we live our lives primarily on the East/West axis. The focus and concentration that we use to create takes us out of the mundane and provides a respite from our daily cares. Intuitively, my father understood that and thus after a work day in which he witnessed terrible suffering, he balanced that experience with creation, creating things in his workshop and creating good in relationships.

Hobbies such as those I saw at the 'Ex' require discipline and attention in order to accomplish them. Knitting is one with which I am familiar. My mother is a master knitter and so she taught me how to knit. I have knit afghans, sweaters, scarfs, mittens and gloves. What I enjoy about knitting is the act itself, the repetitive in and out of the needles, the wool as it slips across my hands, the counting and the pleasure of watching something evolve as I continue. My mind gradually stills as I quietly sit and hear only the click of the needles. In many ways, knitting is a meditative practice, not that different from contemplating a mantra. Indeed, most creative projects are such. One does not learn to play a musical instrument, for example, without discipline and attention. Nor does one build a ship in a bottle or create origami or learn to ballroom dance without them. And the fact that these bring the creator joy is equally important.

The other aspect of creation that is also important is that something is being created and brought into physical form. Necessarily, then, it belongs on the North/South axis. When one, for example, makes Christmas puddings to give to friends as gifts, one brings into the physical something that previously wasn't there. Food, is, of course, very special in this regard for not only do the vitamins and minerals in it nourish us, but so does the love the preparer puts into it. Even teenagers know this. When my son was in high school, I very faithfully made him a lunch every day. I normally put in a couple of interesting sandwiches, usually on buns, as well as fruit and some home baking. I had this idea that somehow my love went along with him to school and that, when he ate the food I was preparing, he was taking in my love. Sometimes I wondered if he ate these lunches. One day, he reported to me that he could have made extra money at school that day. One of the students offered to buy his lunch. He commented that this was not the first time that one of his friends had wanted to eat his lunch. Nor was it the first time he had been offered money for it. I was flabbergasted and delighted to hear that "No way is anyone else eating my lunch."

We ourselves feel that what we are doing is just a drop in the ocean. But if that drop was not in the ocean, I think the ocean would be less because of the missing drop. I do not agree with the big way of doing things.

— *Mother Teresa*

Mother Teresa's contribution was enormous and it was done for one person at a time. But she kept doing it, over and over and over again. If we decide to reclaim beauty as part of our daily lives, the effect on ourselves and others will occur when we do it again and again and

again. That is, it is the doing that matters. Making an interesting and desirable lunch for my son seemed like such a little thing at the time I was doing it. I had no idea if it mattered to him. I just believed that it was important to us. It was some months later that he told me how much he valued it. One does not know how one's acts of beauty affect others, nor even whom. One must simply trust. It is an action one must take in the physical, and yet where it works is the invisible.

The Courage to Create Beauty

Although we don't often think of it this way, creating our own beauty takes enormous courage. First, it takes courage to look into ourselves to find what we want to do, what makes our spirit sing. Second, it takes courage to learn whatever we have to in order to do it. Third, it takes courage to stick to it and complete what we have begun. And finally, it takes courage to present our offerings to the world.

When I was teaching at a community

college, I had a student who had so much courage she left me and her fellow students breathless. This young woman had a dream to go to university. She was smart and talented and knew exactly what she wanted to do. She had enrolled in a course which I offered which was designed to develop students' creativity. In this course, the final project was one which each student devised for himself. Students were required to challenge themselves with something that they really wanted to do but which they were uncertain they *could* do. In her case, she decided that she would apply and get accepted into university. Now, this may not seem like much, but let me tell you a little about her.

She was a second-generation welfare mother. She lived in assisted housing with two children and a boyfriend. She was overweight and terribly shy. And she was brilliant. She came to every class and quietly went about doing her project. At the end of the semester each student was required to present his project to the class in whatever state of completion it was in. I will never forget her presentation. She stood at the front of the class and began taking off her clothes. In fact, she took off layer upon layer of clothing until this beautiful, slender woman appeared in a pair of jeans and a blouse. We were completely shocked. Then she told us her story.

Before she applied to university, she visited the campus. She looked around and realized that none of the other students looked like her. They were, to her eyes, all much, much thinner than she was. She decided that if she was going to go there, she first of all, needed to look like them. So, she put herself on a diet. But, she did not want the class to know, so she kept wearing her shapeless clothes. Then she went on to explain that her friends, her family and her boyfriend were all really upset that she did this. Furthermore, they thought her idea of going to university was ridiculous. As she talked, I realized what she would be doing by going to university. She was going to lose the support of her family, her friends and probably her relationship. To reach her goal, she was going to have to give up the life she knew completely. Moreover, she would be giving up all her training as a welfare child. But she had two children and she wanted a different life for them. And she had a burning inner fire that wanted to express itself. She wanted her brilliance to be in use. And so, she was willing to give up her past and her relationships to express that.

At that moment I realized how easy my life had been. While going to school was hard, for me it was nothing compared to this young woman. All my friends went on to post-secondary education. It was what you did. There was no resistance to doing it. But here was a young woman who had to do it completely alone. Even today, I can only imagine what courage that took. But what beauty we all experienced that day. To a student, there wasn't a dry eye in the classroom.

In fact, there were many beautiful

stories that came out of that class. Student after student overcame enormous obstacles to complete their chosen projects. But the glorious joy each one experienced in the end was magnificent to behold. And I learned that young people welcome the opportunity to look into the self and express what they find there. Given the opportunity, they will step into their power. We must never under-estimate their courage, tenacity and capacity for creating beauty. Nor should we under-estimate our own.

Finding Where the Spirit Sings

There is no perfect way to find out what is inside of us that wants to come out. Everyone does it differently. That I am a jeweler today came about quite by accident. We had moved to a new city where I couldn't find work. I had three teenage children at home and my husband was on the road. I realized that I needed to do something or I was about to become a grumpy person. So I looked over the night school offerings and quite arbitrarily decided on jewelry making. I thought,

"That might be interesting." When I arrived at the school and found the room, I was amazed to find I was in the Industrial Arts room, the room we girls weren't allowed in when I was in school. I was more than a little intimidated. The teacher was brilliant. She immediately got us working with metal. We had to saw a shape. I knew immediately that I wanted to do this. I loved it. As a child, I had always loved building things although I had completely forgotten that. Here I was doing 'carpentry' on metal: sawing, drilling, shaping. It was fabulous.

Three things are important here. First, I recognized that I needed to do something. Second, I acted on that knowledge and simply chose something. Third, I was lucky enough to recognize that I had fallen in love with what I was doing. It does not always happen as easily as that but more often than not, I think it does. The spirit is in some ways a mystery and it does call to us. If we follow that calling, it is very likely that we will find the perfect form of expression for us. It is often tricky because we have to go through the intimidation factor of trying something new. I had to go to metal supply stores, jewelry supply houses and even a place that sells acetylene. These places are full of tools and men. They are not traditional feminine territory. They are very, very industrial. Every single time I opened the door to one of these places, I had to swallow and gather my courage. Although I had a list of tools or materials I needed, I was very aware of my ignorance.

And most of the time I was terrified. But somehow the fire within was strong enough that I was willing to risk my fear and embarrassment. I was always treated very well and eventually I felt quite comfortable buying acetylene, metals and tools. But the process was never even and using the new equipment was tricky. Even though I really wanted to explore a specific piece of equipment, it usually sat on my table for three or four weeks before I would venture to use it. It was like I had to feel it belonged in my studio before I could use it. I am not, by any stretch, the type of person to forge ahead unabashed. I am more the type to dip a big toe in the water, then out, then all toes, then out, then up to the ankle and so on. Other people love to jump right in. The important thing to know is that there is no right way of finding what you want to create. There is only your way.

Learning to Create

The learning process is fraught with difficulties. Above all, we have to get used to failure. I cannot tell you how many pieces of silver have landed in the refuse bin. Or how many designs just don't sell no matter how much I like them. Even today, after years of making jewelry and the creation of a successful business, I still fail. Recently, I was soldering a piece and made a big fat hole in the silver. I can't remember the last time I did such a stupid thing but nevertheless, failure

happens again and again. As I understand it Thomas Edison had 3,000 failures before he created the light bulb. Imagine, 3,000 failures! But this is not something we don't know and have never experienced. Each one of us learned to walk. To do so, we stood up and fell down. Again and again and again. Just remember the explosion of joy that happens the first time a child walks five steps or so. That experience of pure joy occurs every time we learn something we really want to know. It is thrilling. It is beautiful. It takes courage and enormous stubbornness to learn something new. But the result is well worth the journey.

Completing What We Begin

We have lots of experience completing things. But normally these are mundane tasks that have to get done like vacuuming the carpet or preparing dinner or doing the laundry. Each of these things has its own kind of beauty and the completion of such tasks is usually quite satisfying. Just the other day I was telling a friend of mine what a great morning I had. I had a list of errands I needed to complete and spent the morning crossing each errand off my list as I completed it. At the end, I felt a wonderful sense of satisfaction.

Completing a project that we have created for ourselves is a great deal more difficult to do than, for example, washing the car. It is not so much that it is more complicated (though it often is) but rather that we are doing it to express ourselves. Mundane matters frequently take over and we find ourselves postponing that which we do for ourselves. This is where it is really important to remember that part of being human is to experience and nurture our spirits. If we want to have balanced lives, those actions which nourish the spirit are essential.

But knowing that and doing it are two different things. Expressing our creativity is a doing. One can't just think about it and expect it to magically happen. The joy that is available to us through it is only available if we do it. I am very lucky to have a mother who stubbornly completes everything she starts. We have a beautiful wool carpet in our living room that she spent two long winters creating. I marvel at her stubbornness and determination. She suffers from macular degeneration and is now blind in one eye and rapidly losing vision in her other eye. However, on hearing that her grandson was getting married, she decided to knit him and his bride an afghan. It is about half-completed now, but I have no doubt it will be ready for the wedding. I think about all the hours of work that are going into this and how much love my son and soon-to-be daughter-in-law are about to receive. It is beautiful.

In any case, I am very lucky to have a model of completion in my life. When I was a child and I decided to make something, it was never an option in my family to put a project down before it was done. Completing what you start was highly valued in my family. It was a kind of integrity, a keeping of one's word to oneself. This is one of the most difficult of things. Mundane matters frequently intervene when we are creating out of our spirits. The shopping needs to be done. The car needs to be serviced. The dog needs to be walked. And all of these concerns are real to us. So, we put off planting our orchids or playing the piano. And so we deny ourselves the joy of spirit expression.

The other thing that stops us is our own attack thoughts against ourselves. This is the chatter of the mind again and again drawing us back to the East/West axis of the mundane. Our mind tells us that this isn't good enough, or no one will like it, or whose idea was this, anyhow? It points out how many other more important things there are to do and how insignificant our contribution is. Or it might tell us we never finish things so why start now? Any one of these attack thoughts can be true if we make them so. The point is, we made the attack thoughts up in the first place. We are, therefore, quite capable of unmaking them. They are our thoughts. Just because our thoughts will go out and find evidence for us to justify them, doesn't mean we have to react to them by standing at attention and saluting. We can simply say to these pesky mosquito ideas, "Thank you very much for sharing. I am going to work with my orchids now." Eventually, the resistance will stop. However, it might take years before it does. I have just noticed that after four years of doing yoga every morning, my mind, in the past month, has stopped resisting.

One of the beautiful ways of overcoming resistance is to enlist a support person in your project. Tell someone about your project and, if you think it will help you, ask that person to, every once in a while, ask how you are doing at it. Now when you tell them, do so with all the passion that brought you to the project in the first place. This is what will enroll them to support you. For, nothing is more attractive than a spirit that is inspired. This can be one of the things that may be all the difference between you starting something and you finishing it. I have a friend who has supported me through the writing of this book simply by asking me how I am doing every single time we talk together. And I get to respond by telling the truth: "Oh, today, it is the pits. I am in the *aargh* stage of writing" or "It is coming along very well indeed." We rarely talk about the details. Just having that interested party over there seems to lend some kind of credibility to my efforts. I do not feel alone.

Offering to the World

Let's say you choose a project; you prevail over all resistance to your project and you actually complete it. Then what? Well, then it is time to offer it to the world. This is an essential part of the process and I encourage you to do so. Now, if you are really shy, the audience could simply be your cat. But nevertheless, it is important that you present your accomplishment publicly. Remember that beauty and joy lie on the body/spirit axis, that an essential part of creation is bringing the

thing into the physical. An essential part of completion is to offer your contribution to the world. In so doing, you are making a statement about the value of your effort and you find yourself experiencing the joy of creation. My students were always nervous about presenting their projects to the class. Mostly, I think, they were afraid of ridicule. But never once did that happen. Instead, there were tremendous rounds of applause, whistling and stamping, frequently tears and often, hugs. It was glorious and we would all emerge from the classroom ecstatic and inspired.

It takes enormous courage to announce that you are going to take on a project of the spirit. It takes courage to do what has to be done to complete the project. And it takes courage to present your gift of beauty to the world. But the opportunity is to experience the joy of being and to bring that joy to others.

Beauty and Imagination

The thing that ultimately separates us from the rest of the animal kingdom is, of course, our imaginations. This is where so much creativity comes from, imagining what could be. As children, we are brilliant at this. As adults, we are equally brilliant at it. But unfortunately, that brilliance is applied in a different way.

When we are children, we dig holes to China, we build forts out of blankets and chairs, we become movie stars when we try on Mom's high heels. Anything is possible. When my son caught a burr on his pants, instead of being annoyed and brushing it off as I might have, he said, "Oh, look. He is coming for a ride with me!" He was delighted. My son was not concerned that it might damage the fabric of his pants. Nor was he concerned that it might scratch him. He was, instead, delighted to pick up this little hitchhiker. I remember being charmed at the moment, realizing that I would never have made that imaginative leap. But lately, I have been finding myself making just such imaginative leaps and I have discovered they are enormous fun. I am not sure if it is because I have become a grandmother or if I have gained some wisdom. What I do know is that these leaps in imagination produce great joy and even moments of unbounded hilarity. And I know that we adults can all do it.

If you recall, earlier I mentioned that only two percent of adults test as highly creative. Within the scope of the tests, that is probably true. But it is not true that we have lost our creativity. We simply apply it differently. Life as an adult seems to be serious. We have children to care for and protect. We have made investments in mortgages that require us to make sure we can meet our payments. We take on a variety of responsibilities in the workplace. Then we begin to become concerned that we can manage all these simultaneous responsibilities. And because they are important to us, we begin to do something that did not occur to us as children. We worry. We think of what could happen if we don't have the income to support all that we have committed to. That action of worry is a leap of the imagination. Nothing has happened. In the Now, everything is just as we intended it to be. It is only in our imaginations that things go wrong. And yet we believe these imaginings are real. This is no different from the child who believes his blanket and chair are a fort. It is as much of a creative leap to think things could go wrong

as it is to believe the game we created as a child is real.

We are well-supported in these imaginative leaps. We read about how we need to set money aside in order to have a secure retirement. We hear that large companies have gone out of business and that thousands of workers are unemployed. We discover that some bosses steal from their companies. We learn that there are sexual predators on the streets, that there are not enough police or that children get killed playing road hockey. There is a great deal of apparent evidence that the world is a dangerous place, and to that information we apply our very active imaginations. And then we begin to live our lives as if our imaginings are so. This is exactly what we did as children.

When I first began to sell my jewelry, I contracted to sell it from a cart at a large high-end mall. For two weeks, I sold my jewelry to passers-by. My cart was situated about 100 feet from a jewelry store. One afternoon, I heard what I thought was a pop gun and I was thinking to myself, who would bring a child with a pop gun in here? Then I noticed people were running. I still couldn't figure out what was going on. The mall was very, very quiet. Then, suddenly two men dressed in mechanic's coveralls and wearing ski masks came running out of the jewelry store. They went right past me and out a side door. I then realized that a robbery had been going on and was amazed at my naïveté. But still there was no sound in the mall. I looked around and could see no one. Then, another masked figure appeared, this one carrying a gun. He ran no more than ten feet past me and out the door.

Immediately, the mall world changed. Policeman by the dozen appeared. My heart was racing but I thought it was all pretty interesting. Adjacent to me, a young woman also had a cart. She came running out of a nearby store in tears. She was sobbing. I ended up holding her as she cried and cried. Then a television reporter came up to us and wanted to interview the witnesses. I remember being fascinated by him because he looked so odd. It was only later that I realized that he looked so odd because he was wearing so much make-up. Meanwhile, the police were marvelous. They were very kind to everyone — all the shopkeepers, any customers and especially to the young girl I was holding. I remember tapping a policeman on the back to ask where I was supposed to put the witness sheet I had been writing and being completely shocked that he was wearing body armor. I think I jumped about a foot when I realized that.

I was taken upstairs and was interviewed by a female detective. I had drawn a picture of the gun I had seen because I had no idea how one describes a gun. The only gun I had ever seen was my father's revolver and that was not what the young man was carrying. I remember her saying, "You drew the gun. You drew the gun." I was kind of embarrassed because it wasn't a really good drawing but I didn't know how to describe it in any other way and I told her so. She said, "Now, I don't want to upset you, but was it like this?" And she opened her jacket and pulled out a gun. It was just like the one I had seen.

The whole experience of the robbery was fascinating. But the feeling that I had afterwards was one of safety. The police were so kind and caring that that is what I remember most about the experience. Of course, coming from a family of policemen, I have a bias in favor of them. However, I have always been intimidated by the uniform. And I had read as much press as anyone else about police brutality. But this experience was so completely counter to the newspaper accounts of police that I felt I had to do something in support of them. So, what I did do was write the detective (she had given me her card) to ask her to let her superiors know how kind all the policeman had been to us. Not long after, I received a letter from the Chief of Police thanking me for my kind words. He commented that very few civilians ever encounter what I had at the mall that day.

There are several interesting things to say about my perception of the robbery. First, although the young woman at the adjacent cart and I had exactly the same experience, her response was completely different from mine. Where I felt protected and cared for and never felt in danger, she was terrified and never came back to the mall again. And yet, neither of us was harmed. Our imaginations took the experience and made something very different out of it. I was left with a feeling of security while she was left with a feeling of vulnerability. Furthermore, I believe the police chief's words to be true. Very few people ever experience what I did. So why is there so much fear about crime? Because our imaginations take information that we receive and make things of it. There is experience and information and there is what we make of it. That process of making something of it is our imaginations at work.

We do it. It is our doing.

Most frequently, what adults do is take experience and information and transform that into attack thoughts, attack thoughts against others and ultimately attack thoughts against themselves. Without question, it is attack thinking which is the greatest block to experiencing beauty. When we use our imaginations to create attack thoughts, we live life in fear rather than live life in beauty. I found the actions of the police to be beautiful in the aftermath of the robbery and that is where I put my attention. The young woman beside me chose to inflect her experience with her fear of harm and that is where she put her attention. *Even though no harm came to her!* She used her imagination to inflect her perception with fear. Thus she had attack thoughts against herself. She limited her experience. I enriched mine.

Of all the things we do to interfere with our experience of joy and beauty, attack thoughts are probably the most powerful. Let me give you a very simple example. When my elder middle son was six years old, we taught him how to play cribbage. Nobody in the family could beat him. Not because we gave him good cards. We very quickly discovered that there was no need. It was because he was entirely in the game. In the game of cribbage, a hand of four points is a very poor hand. But when he would get a hand of four, he was as delighted as if he had a hand of twenty-four. With complete delight, he would put his cards on the table and then, lifting both arms in the air, with great joy, shout, "I've got four!" And no one could beat him, not even the oldest and most experienced. It was fabulous. When we old and experienced folk would get four, by the way, we would often throw the cards down on the table and groan something like "Ugh, I only have four." This behavior of his is part of our family's lore and still today when my mother and I play, on the occasion of getting four, one or the other of us will throw up our hands in the air and shout, "I've got four!" And then we laugh and laugh and every time, we think of that exuberant child. And inevitably, the next hand is much better. But typically, when adults play this game (except those who know about attack thoughts), they are disgusted with a count of four and the more disgusted they are, the more low-scoring hands they get. I sometimes think the cards do not like to be attacked or, if not the cards, the Card Diva.

Now, you may think this is fanciful thinking and you might be correct. Joy and beauty are fanciful things. If we want to experience them, we have to go there. But especially, we have to give up attack thinking. In an earlier chapter where I introduced the notion of attack thoughts, I suggested a good place to begin taking note of such thoughts is when we are driving. Once you have begun to unravel the many attack thoughts you use against other drivers, you can then move on to notice the ones you use against yourself. These are the tricky ones because we are so used to thinking them that we think of them as normal. The noted motivational speaker Tony Robbins suggests that we are motivated either by fear or by love. What I know about myself is that I am motivated by love. Fear is no help to me at all. Critical judgments towards me always stop me cold. But the critical judgments that most harm me are the ones that I give myself. Thoughts like "What a dummy you are, Kate" or "They will never buy this" or "What made you think you could do that?" are the kinds of self-talk many of us do to ourselves more often than we would like to admit. In fact, we do it often enough that we don't notice doing it. These are attack thoughts based in our imaginations. They are 'what if' kinds of thoughts that have no basis in experience. And yet, we let them steal our power and deprive us of the joy and beauty that are our natural inheritance.

I do not believe that we came to the planet to suffer. Rather, we came here to celebrate the joy of creation and to perceive our relationship with the Creator. To do that, we need to use our imaginations in the way they were intended to be used. Our imaginations can be the doorway we step through to receive the beauty all around us. Or we can use them to slam the door and keep beauty at a distance. The interesting thing is that we all, as children, quite naturally found joy and beauty through our imaginations. So, we do know how to find beauty. It is the willingness that is at issue here.

One day, I was enjoying my normal walk along the seawall to the ferry. It was a gorgeous day — sunny, warm with only a whisper of a breeze off the ocean. Just ahead of me was a young couple with their young daughter. I would say she was at least three years old. Now, nothing is more magical than a three-year-old and here she was in the sunshine, beside the ocean holding her father's hand. Her father leaned over and said, pointing to the dock, "See that pretty boat? Do you want to take a ride on the boat?" He was engaging her imagination and creating anticipation for something wonderful ahead. At that moment, I passed the couple by. Almost immediately, I heard the woman say, "Would you please not use your electric toothbrush at night when I am in bed trying to sleep? Do you have any idea how annoying that is? And stop slamming the bathroom door." I couldn't believe I was hearing this. What did any of that have to do with the beautiful morning and the adventure the little girl was about to enjoy? Where was the magic of the day? Where was the joy of it? When we are trapped in the past and have no awareness of the present around us, we are using our imaginations to describe something that no longer exists. We are choosing to ignore the beauty of creation and the many gifts in front of us. The time to complain about a noisy toothbrush is when it is being noisy, when both parties are in the experience. Otherwise, what is being discussed is only a story and such a disconnected story from the present experience available that it is unlikely that anything will come of the complaint. This is, of course, a young woman choosing to live her life on the East/West axis, the axis of the mundane. And memory and imagination took her there. Her attack thoughts were directed outwards towards her husband. She could have instead, easily in the circumstances, chosen to experience the joy and wonder of the North/South axis. She did not. And every single one of us has done a similar thing at one time or another. If we are not happy, it is because we choose not to be. Joy is always available.

About three minutes later, I was walking down to the ferry. When I got to it, it looked like the ferry was full. This was not, of course, in the least upsetting to me as standing on a floating dock, waiting for the next ferry, gazing at the ocean and the mountains behind is one of my favorite things, so I was quite willing to wait. But the young man who runs the ferry said, "There is enough room and you can get on if you would like." I chose to do just that as I had been dallying this morning and wanted to get to the studio. I stepped on to the ferry and looked to the right and the left. To the right were a motley group of men, women and children. To the left were a large group of women. As soon as I looked to the left, the women as one, all moved and made a space for me. It was graceful and generous of them and sweepingly beautiful. "Ah!" I thought to myself. "Life is beautiful." After I thanked the women, we proceeded to have a lovely trip across to the island. Of course, this was a very small moment, but it was a beautiful one. And, indeed, experiences of beauty are often small ones but are treasures as great as important works of art. There is no question that the disturbance the young mother created in her comments as I passed her could have disrupted my trip to the studio as my mind could have picked that up and ruminated on it and could have created attack thoughts against her. Instead, I was given the gift of these kind women and my beauty equilibrium was restored. Always, always, always, this is available to us. We just have to choose beauty and receive it.

While receiving beauty is an enormous pleasure, in my experience it is the creation of beauty I find most gratifying. Often the process itself is satisfying. I notice that it is when I am creating new designs that I have the most fun. It is not that I don't like making jewelry, for I feel very lucky to be doing work that I enjoy. It is just that replication is not as mysterious and interesting as designing it. Often when I design, I have several failures before the piece is as I envision it. But I do not find this daunting. Rather, I find it to be exciting. I have come to realize that it is through my failures that I find the most beautiful work. The failures are pathways to beauty. Always, during the periods when I am creating my new lines, I find myself to be excited and engaged. I am never happier in my work. The other part is the more I create, the more I create.

Take the writing of this book, for example. I like writing. Indeed, I always have. Though I don't remember, my mother tells me that I was often writing as a child. For many years, I taught writing and, while I did some writing myself, when I was teaching I was more pre-occupied with raising my family than writing. The thing that has surprised me about writing this book is that the more I write, the more I want to write. I have a friend who lives a long way away from me and we manage to see each other about twice a year. In between visits, we normally either telephone or e-mail. Recently I decided that, instead of e-mailing him, I would write. Well, that turned out to be an amazing adventure. In the middle of the letter, I created the most outrageously ridiculous story you can imagine. In fact, it was exactly that, the documentation of an imagining I had one day while standing on the ferry dock. It is both beautiful and ex-ceedingly funny and is way beyond anything I have ever thought up before. My imagination seems to soar when I write him letters and I must say, I can't wait to write the next one. Two things about this. Until I wrote him, I hadn't realized how much I enjoy writing. Secondly, I accessed a part of myself that is a deeply funny, joyful person. Now that I have found her, I am very clear that she has to continuously express herself. So I guess more letters will just have to be written.

But it is always that way with creative projects. When I was first married, I knew nothing about cooking. I had once baked a cherry pie and that was all I knew about cooking. Realizing that we couldn't very well live on cherry pies, I purchased a couple of cookbooks and began the process of learning how to cook. It was a fascinating process and a great deal of fun. Eventually, I got to the point that I was giving five-course dinner parties for eight from scratch including making my own bread. It was wonderful.

But that is the thing about our creativity — once we tap into it, it is like pulling a string. We just have to keep going for as long as the string will go. But what is even better is that when we create beautiful things, we are inspired and joy just bubbles up through us and overflows. Living our lives through the beauty we create is just such a satisfying thing to do. It is a kind of joyful giving. And I am inclined to think that that is just what the Creator intended.

Conscious Acts of Beauty

Too late came I to love thee, O thou Beauty both
so ancient and so fresh, yea too late came I to love
thee. And behold, thou wert within me, and I
out of myself, where I made a search for thee.
                    — *St. Augustine, Confessions*

*T*he secret to making beauty is to understand that it comes from within each of us. While we may think that we cannot ever be a Michelangelo, we must remember that we were never intended to be. We were intended to be ourselves. That is what our beauty is. A conscious act of beauty is an action that is taken in the physical world that expresses some kind of inner truth. It is a doing. And more often than not it is a little doing. Its purpose is to express inner beauty and to enroll others in the experience of that.

Let us say you are preparing dinner. You are married with two children, both teenagers. You have had a very busy day at the office. Your husband has arrived home tired and frustrated. He brought home his laptop and is working at his desk. Your children are surly and are supposed to be doing homework. There you are, alone in the kitchen making a salad to go along with the lasagna that you made on the weekend. You wonder to yourself, "Why do I do this? Why do I go to so much trouble when they will wolf down the food and be away from the table in five minutes?" You are in danger of coming to the table as grumpy as they all seem to be. Then you think of dinner conversation, such as it is. You don't really want to know how nasty the math teacher is or how annoying your husband's staff is. You think, "How can I change this? What can I do to elevate dinner conversation?"

You decide to make an experiment. You find some beautiful bright pink napkins in a drawer. You fold them into fans and you place them on each of the plates on the table. It took you less than five minutes to do so. Then you call everyone to the table for dinner. One by one they wander in. "Oh," says your daughter, "is it somebody's birthday?" "What's this for?" says your son. "Mmm, that's nice," comments your husband.

What you have created is an opening, an opening to the vertical axis where a level of conversation outside of the mundane can occur. You might mention that you are grateful that you can all be together and just wanted to show that appreciation in some way, that you thought the family deserved to celebrate itself. Or you might talk about making the table more beautiful, that more beauty is important. Or you might say you always liked fans and thought it would be fun to make some. You have interrupted the normal pattern of dinner conversation and in so doing, you have made it possible to communicate with each other more deeply.

It is possible that nothing will happen, that nobody will notice the action you have taken. Do not be discouraged about that. Conscious acts of beauty do make an impact. I need only think of my grandmother's family dinners to know that they had an impact on me. More than half a century has passed since I attended one and the memories are clear and vivid. It was a couple of months of making my son's lunches before he commented on them to me. I had to trust that they mattered. In a sense, conscious acts of beauty are the art of living.

Filling a space in a beautiful way. That's what art means to me.

— *Georgia O'Keefe*

A conscious act of beauty fills space in a beautiful way. One very simple way of filling space in a beautiful way is to become conscious of what we say. The English language is a beautiful one, but in day-to-day speech, it is rarely used in a beautiful way. Instead of describing our experience explicitly, we use meaningless words like 'great' or 'boring'. It is often difficult to express in language what our experience is. For English operates in a linear way whereas experience occurs simultaneously. That is, at the same time I am reviewing a report, I might also notice the drone of an airplane in the background as well as the whirring of the air conditioning system as well as my neighbor's conversation with a co-worker and I may see the overhead light flickering and smell coffee as someone passes my doorway. I may notice that my back is aching and I may remember that it is my daughter's birthday and I had better remember the birthday cake. Experience is rich and varied with enormous depth to it. Whenever we speak of our experience, it is unlikely that we are ever going to convey all of it. Thus, we must edit it and choose what we will express of it. How sad that we edit into meaningless phrases the richness of our experience.

"I felt manacled to my chair as I reviewed the profitability reports. I would rather have followed the aroma of the coffee that was being carried down the hall by Theresa." Although such a comment does not depict the entire experience the individual was having, there is a richness in the communication that reveals depth. Many of us have developed patterns of speech that much of the time have no meaning whatever. The inner self is not being expressed yet again. When one considers that the largest vocabulary of any language is contained in English, it is rather sad that we choose to use the language in such mundane ways. Imagine what would happen to our conversation if people accurately described their experience. Of course, for most of us it would mean keeping a thesaurus in our hip pocket or the *Oxford English Dictionary of Quotations* on our desk, but why not? It could be fun. That is the thing about conscious acts of beauty. They are often fun.

Joy is the dynamic aspect of Being. When the creative power of the universe becomes conscious of itself, it manifests as joy.

— *Eckhart Tolle*

When I went away to nurse's training, my grandfather moved into my room. My mother tells me that every day at 3:45, he took out the cribbage board and the playing cards and set them on the kitchen table. When my brother arrived home from school, the contest began. My grandfather was an expert cribbage player. He taught my brother everything he knew about the game. But was it work? Absolutely not. Apparently, the games were raucous. My brother would accuse Grandpa of cheating. With a twinkle in his eye, Grandpa would deny it. My brother, David, would get louder and my grandfather would laugh harder. To this day, my brother gets pleasure from the memory of those games. Were these acts of beauty? Well, if joy and laughter and forging a relationship count, they certainly were. Did they come from the inner self? The intention of my grandfather to 'play' with his grandson was certainly conscious. The joy with which my brother remembers these times seems to me to be a testament to their power.

At this time in my life, my mother is living with me. Well into her eighties, she is lively and sharp. Now, each evening after supper, we play cribbage together. Sometimes we laugh so hard that tears come to our eyes. Sometimes we look up and call on Grandpa to help us (he usually does). When my luck turns downward and in an effort to reverse my bad fortune, I run into the bathroom, touch the bathtub and run back to my chair (a trick my father taught me). This makes my mother explode into laughter and, inevitably, it brings me a high-scoring hand. Recently, a friend of mine was visiting and she joined in our cribbage games. As I was driving her to the airport, she commented on the cribbage games and on the 'beautiful' relationship I have with my mother. For not only do we laugh and tease each other in the games, but we also laugh a great deal the rest of the time. Cribbage seems to have taught us how to have a joyous, loving relationship together. It is a conscious act of beauty.

The older I get the less I think 'important' things matter and the more I think joy matters. Have you noticed that when you laugh, and I mean really laugh, your mind stops? You aren't thinking when you laugh deeply. You are in the experience of the laughter. One of the most available ways in which we can do conscious acts of beauty is by creating joy, by enrolling others in laughter.

When we do that, the lightness of our spirits comes forth. And inevitably it enriches others. I remember years ago knowing a man who was part of a work group to which

I belonged. He was a serious intellectual, an economist with a prodigious intelligence. When Robert spoke, we all paid attention. But there was something else about him that endeared him to us. He had the deepest, heartiest, most rollicking laugh I have ever heard. It seemed to come from deep in his belly, gaining resonance as it moved through his body and finally through his vocal cords. When Robert laughed, his laugh seemed to fill every corner of the room. It seemed to bounce off the walls and ricochet around the room. Everyone laughed with him. It was impossible not to. Today when I think of him, I think not of his brilliance. Rather, I smile to myself as I recall his laughter.

Robert's gift of laughter was a treasure. It saved many a meeting when we were dropping off into boredom or frustration. I have no idea if he knew it was time for a laugh, but I like to think so. I like to think of his laughter as a conscious act of beauty which rescued us from the mire of the East/West axis, bouncing us on to the vertical, getting us in touch with our spirits, balancing the mind work we were doing.

This is perhaps, the most important gift that conscious acts of beauty provide. They give us balance. It is well-known that many difficult and complex scientific breakthroughs have occurred not in the laboratory, but in the shower or on the golf course. One of the most famous accounts is, of course, Archimedes who, in his bath, jumped up and shouted "Eureka" (I've got it). The intense machinations of the mind have finally let go and in their relaxation, the truth emerges.

We live in a world in which the quantity of information we are sifting through each day is so great that it is virtually impossible to stay current. We are challenged by e-mail, voice mail, blogs, newspapers, books, magazines, reports, presentations, telephone calls, meetings, radio and television. And frequently, information is coming to us through three or more channels at one time. This is a kind of information insanity that the world has never seen before. The information highway is one huge traffic jam and it is wearing us down. Tempers are short, anxiety abounds and cool, rational thought is disappearing. Leaders have become reactive rather than proactive.

Recently, I was speaking with a management consultant who travels the world, working with and speaking to senior managers. His observation of corporate life is worrisome: "CEO's and their senior managers are so overwhelmed with the quantity of information coming to them that they have no time to think. Because I am a specialist in strategy, business for me is good. But one has to be concerned when an organization has to hire someone like me to do the thinking for it." When one looks at the number of large organizations that have disappeared over the past several years, one has to wonder if he doesn't have a point.

In order for a business to endure in today's climate, it will likely have to transform itself every five years. Transformation in business does not occur by collecting information. Transformation occurs out of leadership, vision and execution of strategy. But none of these things come out of activity and reaction. These things occur out of stillness and silence, then moving to directed action.

An element of contemplation is absolutely essential in transformation. Butterflies are created out of cocooned caterpillars. A period of withdrawal and silent reflection is an essential ingredient in the transformative process. A stepping out of the mundane is required. Organizations work very well on the horizontal axis. This is the busy-ness of day-to-day tasks. This is answering calls, meeting sales targets, motivational meetings, problem solving, report writing, etc. But no matter how well-oiled the machine of business is, transformation will not occur on the mind/heart axis. What occurs best there is repetitive, prescriptive, reactive behavior.

Typically, organizations are command and

control structures. They are often hierarchical and ultimate responsibility lies with their leaders. If a leader believes that it is his job to keep shareholders happy by keeping profits up, he had better also understand that in today's environment, his product and organization will need to transform completely within five years. To begin with, he will need to find how exactly it will transform. He will not find that by listening to the board, by fighting fires, by reacting to events. Although that is part of his job, his primary work is to lead the organization to the next stage of development so that it prevails ten years hence.

But how does he find the opportunities that will guide him to the next direction for his company? By becoming familiar with the vertical axis, the axis of creativity. One becomes familiar with anything not by occasional contact, but by repeated contact. So, taking the odd seminar or occasionally doing one's favorite pastime is not repeated contact. Living on the vertical axis must be engaged in regularly and repeatedly in order for familiarity to occur.

This means that leaders must devote a period of each day to engaging in actions which move them to the vertical, the timeless. A minimum of 15 minutes each day needs to be devoted to an action which removes one from the mundane, an action which occurs alone and one practiced in silence, an action that moves one towards joy. It is recommended that the action be uniquely one's own. It could be growing orchids, making origami, thinking about the sayings of Plato, contemplating a poem by William Blake, playing a musical instrument, writing in a journal (in the present tense only), doing some yoga postures, walking in a garden, painting watercolors, practicing calligraphy or any action which makes the spirit sing. The idea is that one's attention is focused on an action which absorbs one enough that time drops away.

Such behaviors remove one from the mundane and make room for creative energy

to open up. Although one is concentrating on something completely unrelated to one's 'work', this is often what is essential in finding a creative solution to a difficult situation.

We have all had the experience of, for example, trying to untie a shoelace that has become irrevocably knotted. We pull and push and manipulate, gritting our teeth, breaking a fingernail and still are unable to loosen it. Then we put it down, 'give up'. A few hours later, we pick up the shoe and undo the knot — without thinking, without effort. Often, letting go of the cares of the day is the best way to find the answer.

But, for a leader who must create and lead his organization in a new direction, setting aside time each day to step off the mundane is really a primary directive. If he doesn't do this, he will have to hire someone like my friend to make the crucial insights needed. This is not always the best thing for one's organization or even one's career.

Promise To Do a Conscious Act of Beauty

What I encourage each one of us to do is to make a promise to the self to perform one conscious act of beauty every day. I recommend formalizing this promise by writing it down, signing it and then posting it somewhere where you will encounter it daily.

Remembering that the vertical axis is comprised of the physical as well as the spiritual, it is crucial that you write down your promise and sign it. Take your promise out of your mind and make it physically real.

This will help you in keeping your word to yourself and it will alert the universe that you are serious. Each time you see your promise, you will be reminded of it and that reminder will encourage you to take action.

Start small. Perhaps you will decide to make a conscious act of beauty in the interpersonal domain. An opportunity will come up to smile at someone and give him a compliment. Perhaps you decide to make a conscious act of beauty in the personal domain and so you decide to wear a favorite piece of jewelry, one you love but rarely wear. Perhaps you decide to print out a favorite photo of an object you admire and tack it to your desk. Perhaps you decide to take your lunch break and walk to a neighboring park to enjoy the spring flowers. Remember that the conscious act of beauty is something that you do for yourself. It is a promise you give yourself to access your spirit every day. It can be the smallest thing that no one else knows you are doing. I recall signing my divorce papers at my lawyer's office one day. As I was doing it, I glanced up and looked out the window. In the sky was a rainbow. For just a moment, I stopped and enjoyed it. My lawyer didn't notice. Only I did. That experience of beauty was a blessing to me for at that moment I was signing documents that would be irrevocably changing my life.

The Power of a Practice

What you are doing when you keep your promise of a conscious act of beauty a day is known as a practice. It is a repetitive action designed to inflect spirit into your life. The keeping of a journal is also a practice. Practice is one of the most ancient of behaviors and one of the most powerful. We have all heard of meditation and yoga as practices. But many of us do not realize that we engage in practices every day. The gardener who walks through her garden every day, perhaps touching this plant or that, perhaps bending over to clear some debris is practicing receiving the beauty she has created. The long-distance runner who runs five miles every day is performing a practice. The mother who kisses her children before they leave for school is performing a practice. The individual who silently blesses the food he is about to eat is performing a practice. The musician who picks up his instrument every day and plays (no matter how long) is performing a practice. The businessman who writes thank-you notes to clients is performing a practice. But all of these actions are practices only if they are done consciously.

If I peck my child's cheek out of habit, I am not performing a practice. Instead, I am engaged in patterned behavior. This is behavior of the mind. It is comprised of musts and shoulds, of expectations and memories. The mind operates out of habits. Decisions are made, often when we are very young, and ever after, we respond in a specific way to a particular circumstance. This is akin to how a computer works. It performs according to its programming. Much of the dissatisfaction experienced in our lives occurs because instead of taking conscious actions, we are operating out of habit. Thus we have difficulty experiencing the joy, for joy which is found on the spirit/body axis, not on the mind/heart axis.

The crucial part of performing a practice is choice. One consciously chooses to take action. It does not come out of habit. And each time one does the practice, he chooses to do it. Again and again and again. This is no small thing because the opposition of both the mind and those around us can be overwhelming. I recall talking to a marathon runner who, as much as she loved to run, found that every day she could find a reason not to run. Her mind would remind her she didn't have enough time or she was too tired or the weather wasn't very good (mentally promising it would be better later on) or she really ought to get new running shoes. There were hundreds of reasons not to run. And she chose to do it every day in spite of the mind's interruptions. Any one of the reasons the mind served up could be construed as true. Nevertheless, my friend ran every day. And she gloried in it.

The other resistance to performing a practice often comes from those around us. This opposition to what we are doing is not personal in the sense that it is against us. It is really resistance to the interruption of the normal pattern of behavior that exists in the relationship. Intuitively, we all know that when a member of the family takes up a practice, we are all going to be affected. If, for example, one decides to go for a walk each morning before breakfast, then the waking and breakfast routine are going to be interrupted and some uncertainty will enter in. It is the uncertainty that is most upsetting to those around us when we make a change. So it is important to understand that people are responding to their own uncertainty not to your action. Simply thank them for letting you know their concern and continue doing your practice. You will be surprised at how quickly they adjust.

I have called this section the power of practice. By 'power', I do not mean control and yet, this is what we commonly mean when we use the word 'powerful'. Most often when we say something like "He is powerful or she has a lot of power," we are actually talking about control. Control is an external attribute. Power implies the internal. Power is when we are in touch with our spirits, especially when we act from there. It means standing in the centre of who we are at our deepest. Control we have over others is irrelevant. Only engagement with the truth of self is relevant.

What is really wonderful about engaging in conscious acts of beauty is that we, in doing whatever it is we choose to do, inform our lives with spirit and so begin to experience our power. And the more we do it, the more likely joy is to emerge.

It will emerge in us and it will emerge in those around us. In my neighborhood is a very special garden. The home owners love to garden and so they have created an abundant and glorious garden in their small front yard and on the adjacent boulevard. The garden is so beautiful that people come out of their way to walk past it. Often, they stop in front of it and simply gaze. It is a treasure in our community and valued by all of us. The owners' joy in their act of beauty is obvious to all of us and each time we walk past it, our spirits are lifted.

Conscious acts of beauty are gifts, gifts to ourselves and gifts to others. They are often small, apparently insignificant doings and yet they can have significant impact. Play with them. Enjoy them. What follows are some possibilities.

25 Conscious Acts of Beauty

1. Compliment someone.

This can be a compliment about appearance, accomplishment, temperament, any number of things. It can be a compliment to a member of the family, a friend, a co-worker or a complete stranger. Give your compliment freely with no expectation of a response. And, to the best of your ability, let that compliment come from your spirit. Let it be a truth for you.

In a notebook, note your reaction to this gift you have given. Perhaps you feel good. Perhaps you feel uncomfortable. Perhaps you have no response at all. Notice, too, how others receive a compliment. Are they able to let it in and simply say 'thank you,' or do they return the compliment to you? For example, the most common return is responding to "I love you" with "I love you, too." When we give a compliment back like that is that we haven't actually received it. Rather, we have deflected it. Remember that being able to receive is a huge part of allowing beauty into our lives. Do not judge your response nor that of she who is receiving it. Simply notice. This is part of the process of becoming conscious.

2. Belly laugh.

Once during the day, bend over and hold your stomach as you laugh deeply. It doesn't matter if there is something to laugh at or not (although it is certainly easier if there is something to laugh at). Really let go. Don't just smile and hold it in. Laugh with all your heart.

Note what happened when you belly laughed. How did you feel? Were you thinking? How about those around you? Did they laugh too or did they walk away or did they simply look at you with a confused expression on their face? Did you notice nothing at all because you were having such a good time laughing that that was all there was? This may seem like a ridiculous conscious act of beauty. But there is no question that the more you laugh, the more you laugh.

3. When your work day is over, change your clothes.

Wear something beautiful, something you treasure. Choose something you rarely wear, but something that makes you feel wonderful, rich and enriched. We all have clothes like this and often don't wear them just because we are being practical. There is nothing more eminently practical than shedding one's work clothes, clothes that hold the memories of boring meetings or surly customers. When one then puts on something that makes him or her feel wonderful, it is likely that the day's challenges retreat and the joy of life moves forward.

I, for example, have a favorite silver belt. When I put it on, I feel beautiful. Even just doing that will change the way I feel and the way I treat myself. Beautiful clothes can be very simple things. They simply need a little swing to them. I am reminded of the Lasse Hallström movie *Chocolat*. There is one camera shot I just love. It is the shot of the three old women all dressed in black walking away from the *chocolaterie*. In synchronous steps, they walk up the street. Hallström has the camera focus on the skirts and we watch them swing from left to right. It is beautiful.

Note your response to changing clothes. Did you feel foolish? Did you feel wonderful? Did your daily frustrations drop away? Did you feel like you ought to be going to a party? Remember, you are *the party.*

4. **Write a thank-you note, on paper, and mail it.**

Make this a personal and authentic

communication. Thank someone for a kindness they have done. Thank someone for a gift. Thank someone for the gift of their friendship. Thank a customer for his business. Thank your dentist for the kindness of his staff. Thank yourself for being you.

Note your response to writing such a letter. Was it fun? Was it difficult? Do you feel satisfied after mailing it?

5. **Smell a flower.**

Move right up to the flower. Allow the velvet soft petals to caress your face. Breathe in.

Document how you felt, what the flower felt like against your skin and to the best of your ability, describe the fragrance you received.

6. **Pick up a piece of trash and place it in an appropriate receptacle.**

The most important thing to do here is to pay attention to how your mind wants to run in this action.

Does it want to create an attack thought

against the person who dropped the trash or does it want to attack you for being silly enough to think your action will make a difference? Or, are you able to simply celebrate the liberation of the grass or sidewalk on which the trash lay?

7. **Consider those things for which you are grateful.**

An excellent place to contemplate gratitude is while you are driving to work. List for yourself all the things for which you are grateful. List family, friends, opportunities, work that you like, hobbies, possessions, pets, anything you have in your life which enriches you and which you treasure. You will be surprised at how generous you feel when you arrive at work.

8. **Give up your place in a line to someone who needs it, perhaps an elderly person, a physically challenged person or a harried young mother.**

To do this, you will have to be on the lookout.

It is surprising how often we do not notice that a simple generous act can create joy.

Record both noticing the need and the effects to you and others of the giving.

9. **Before getting out of bed in the morning, take two minutes to listen to the songbirds outside your window.**

So many of us get up to the sound of an alarm, that we fail to experience the joy that is all around us as Nature greets the day. Taking the time to do so is a delightful way to begin your day with beauty.

10. **Take a fifteen-minute walk in nature.**

Nature is so generous with her beauty that it is always a joy to spend time with her. If you have had a particularly trying day at work, take a break with nature. Feel her caress your skin, the beauty around you and the sounds of joy that come from her. Look for them.

Document your experiences.

11. **Interrupt an attack thought by singing to yourself.**

It takes some time for us to notice our attack thoughts for they sneak up on us in the most subtle of ways and they always seem to be real. But, when you do notice one, the most efficient way of cutting it off is to sing to yourself. You can sing anything. It doesn't matter if it is a down-and-out blues tune or an inspiring hymn or even if it is a nonsense song you make up. Just sing. You will banish the attack thought by doing so.

12. **Plant a butterfly garden.**

Imagine being surrounded by beautiful butterflies. One of the ways to encourage their presence is to have flowers in our gardens that attract them. Any seed store will have seeds that can be planted and grown into flowers that butterflies love.

13. **Create a birthday card and send it.**

If you like computers, find an image that

you love and create a card. My grandchildren love to carve images into potatoes. After applying ink from a pad, they stamp the images onto cards. The most delightful, personal and thoughtful cards show up this way. Remember, though, to send your card. Complete your little project.

Remind yourself by writing about how much fun you had.

14. Make a statement of gratitude before you eat.

Most of us are in a rush a great deal of the time. Thus, when it comes to our meals, we often eat as expediently as possible in unconsciousness. Take a moment to stop, step back, breathe and then, in gratitude, silently thank the food for the nourishment it brings to us.

15. Clean some brass or silver.

Because I am a metal worker, I notice tarnished metals. Clean a tarnished doorknob or handle on a piece of furniture. Watch the sparkle emerge as you do so.

Describe in writing how you feel whenever you notice the now-glistening object in your home.

16. Create your own personal archive of responses to "How are you?"

Have fun with this. Be outrageous.

Notice both how you enjoyed making them up and how people responded to them.

17. Eat a meal in candlelight.

The great joy of candlelight meals is that generally, we slow down when we eat and find ourselves engaging in aroma, texture and taste. These are simple pleasures and bring us in touch with beauty in most surprising ways.

18. Play a game.

It doesn't matter what the game as long as it is for the purpose of the fun of it. Play

Parcheesi, or pick-up-sticks, or hopscotch, or a simple game of catch. See if you can reclaim some of the delight you experienced as a child.

19. Wash the car.

Remember how you loved to wash the car when you were a child? Remember how you used to have water fights when you did so? Why not do that again? Why not get soaking wet? What an opportunity to laugh.

20. Go on a picnic.

Try an old-fashioned picnic with egg salad sandwiches, watermelon, cookies and lemonade. Play spit the seeds. Sit on a blanket and count the ants that visit. Name the clouds that float by.

21. Listen to a favorite piece of music.

Music is perhaps one of the most unlikely creations we humans have produced. It is also among the most inspiring.

Notice how you feel when you hear your favorite piece. Does it relax you? Does it give you joy? Do you find that your thoughts have silenced somewhat? Do you find that now you can tackle that difficult and unpleasant task you have been avoiding? Remind yourself of the effect of listening to music by writing about it.

22. **Write a love letter.**

One of the most beautiful art forms is the love letter. We are in danger of losing this most simple and lovely of communications. Either buy or make some stationery and then put your pen to paper. Write the letter from the present, from where you are. Perhaps reflect on the nature around you or the music you are listening to as you write or even, if you are lucky, the glass of champagne you are drinking. You do not even have to say "I love you". Just concentrate on writing a beautiful message that is exclusively for your loved one. One of the things that is so lovely about love letters is that they are written and sent and then, by the time the recipient gets it, we have often forgotten what we said. It is then a surprise when our loved one responds. How beautiful.

23. **You know that drawer or closet where you store things that you don't need, want or like or even use any more? Clean it. Divest yourself of all the clutter you insist on keeping. Make some space in your life.**

Have fun doing this. Prepare by gathering boxes or bags that are labeled. Either label contents or label delivery location. Perhaps you will have a garage sale. Get a friend to help you. Have a 'clean the closet' party. Make up a trunk of dress-up clothes for a favorite child. Above all, intend for beauty to fill the now-empty space. Record your accomplishment.

24. **Watch the sun set.**

Take the time to be with the sun as it sets. Are you able to simply sit and watch? Find the silence. Enjoy the beauty. Record the experience.

25. **Belly dance.**

To do this, play a favorite piece of music. Roll up your shirt to leave your abdomen bare. Move with the music paying special attention to undulations of the abdomen. Remember that your center is the solar plexus. Belly dancing gives the solar plexus a massage. Enjoy this. Laugh with yourself. Find the lightness of your being. Notice how you feel while doing it and then how you feel afterwards. Record your responses.

Beauty Practices

*P*ractices differ from conscious acts of beauty because they are actions that we take again and again. Their purpose is to provide a context within which spirit can assert itself and so beauty can emerge. Like conscious acts of beauty, these do not have to be complex undertakings. They can be simple doings. But they must be done every day, or at least six out of seven, no matter what. Eventually this may mean you have to make choices and these may feel uncomfortable. Just remember that all those good ideas of other things you could be doing are attack thoughts against yourself. It doesn't matter how reasonable they seem. Remember that the vertical axis is an experience of depth, not of breadth and you must enter it to experience it. Essentially, you have to find the practice that works for you. What follows are suggestions of places you might look to find yours.

1. Start with a physical practice of some kind, remembering that the North/South axis is grounded in the physical. It is important to know your body. I began many years ago walking for twenty minutes once a day. That eventually grew into one hour once a day. I chose a particular route through my neighborhood and always followed that route. At the time, we lived near a long ravine and though I didn't go into the ravine, I felt the benefits of it. For example, I frequently encountered a red fox that clearly lived in the ravine but which would visit the neighborhood. The wonderful thing about walking is

that you usually do it in nature and thus you become connected with the rhythms inherent in her. Today, as you know, I walk back and forth from home to my studio. What is interesting is that on the days that I don't go to the studio, I find that at some point in the day I have to go for a walk. My body and my spirit demand it.

Once you have found a simple practice like walking, you can move on to a body-conditioning practice like yoga or Pilates or dancing or swimming or cycling or kayaking. Whatever takes your fancy. It is likely that you will need to find a teacher, but it is my experience that the perfect one will show up somehow. So my daily physical practices are walking and yoga. I cannot conceive of not doing them anymore. In fact, they are so important to me that I will not attend early morning breakfast meetings. Such gatherings interrupt the well-being I experience by following my morning practice. That is more important to me than any information

I might gather at a meeting. If something is urgent, then I just get up earlier than usual. Under no circumstances do I miss my morning physical practice. You will find, over time, that the same thing will happen to you. My understanding, though, is that it takes a full year for the chemistry of the body to adjust to a physical change. If what you need to do in order to faithfully complete your physical practice each day is to mark off your accomplishment on a calendar, then do so. Whatever works is good. Just do it.

You do not always have to be reflective when doing a practice, but it is interesting to take note of how your mind responds to it. It can take a very long time for the mind to stop its interference. It took me four years. And that is just an opening, for now I can begin my practice without mind interference. During the practice, my mind is as interfering as ever.

2. The oldest and best-documented practice is, of course, meditation. For thousands of years, it has been held as an integral part

of developing an awareness of spirit. There are many forms of meditative practices and many resources available to help you. There are dancing meditations, sitting meditations, singing meditations and even working meditations. My meditation of choice is *A Course in Miracles*. It contains 365 meditations, one for every day of the year. When I complete the series, I begin again. This is a good practice for anyone who has had a Christian upbringing as I did, because the language in it is familiar to those who attended Sunday school or church.

Eckhart Tolle's work *The Power of Now* is another reading that could be used as a meditative practice. He has taken ancient spiritual ideas and translated them into modern language with modern examples. This is the one my mother has chosen.

I have friends who do Zen practices. Others do Buddhist meditations and others First Nations practices. It really depends on what resonates with you. Some people like to

read poetry each morning. But the repeated practice of contemplation and the stillness of the mind that it engenders opens the spirit and makes a pathway that allows you to experience beauty more frequently and more deeply than you have before.

Meditation is, in some ways, completely alien to Western life which is so deeply inflected with activities. If you decide to take it on, do it for long enough and faithfully enough that you can experience a difference in your experience. But do it only if it calls to you. I knew about *A Course in Miracles* for over 25 years before I actually started it. It was a huge emotional upheaval in my life which took me to it. I knew that if I wanted to go through the transition I was facing with grace and come out of it strengthened, I would need some help. *A Course in Miracles* is what I chose and it was perfect for me. But your spirit may move in very different ways and you will need to find what is right for you.

3. Find a hobby that you love to do and do

it each day. This can be anything as long as it is constructive. It can be knitting or sewing, carpentry or gardening, making soap or practicing calligraphy, anything you love to do into which you are absorbed and during which time drops away.

The more you do an action like one of these, an action which inspires you, the more you will come to your own stillness and find the place where your spirit sits. The more you inflect your life with actions of beauty, the more joy will show up.

The Beauty Notebook

What you have just read is my own beauty notebook. This is my journey into beauty. This is my gift to you. I encourage each and every one of you to begin your own beauty notebook. Jot down beautiful things you do and observe. Notice as much as you can about them, how you feel, how others respond, what exactly captures your imagination. Notice those times, too, when you feel your imagination being thwarted and attempt to identify the source of that. Perhaps you will feel moved

to include photographs in your notebook or pressed flowers. Whatever will bring you back to beauty is worth documenting.

Remember that the more beauty you see, the more beauty you see and the more beauty you do, the more beauty you do. This could be the practice you choose. Simply write about beauty in your notebook every day. It doesn't matter if it is two words or two hundred and fifty. It is the repeated doing that will bring beauty back into your life. And that will bring you back onto the North/South axis and into the experience of living a deep and fulfilling life.

Beauty Treasure Box

Do you remember collecting precious things when you were a child? You might find a pretty piece of glass or a special stone or a shiny gum wrapper. I recall when my children were small, forcing myself to check their pockets before I washed their clothes. I was usually worried a snake would show up. The quietest of the three boys was always the one who had interesting things in his pockets. My favorite was the day I found twenty-two acorns.

Mementos of beauty can reignite the joy we experienced in the moment. A stone we picked up on a beach while on vacation, a quotation from a book we read, a paper napkin from an afternoon tea, a pressed flower, the insignia from an old army uniform, a letter from a beloved friend, a faded photograph: all of these can remind us of the beauty that is always available to us. Placing our notebook in a special box reminds us of the precious nature of beauty. That we have allocated a physical location for these things places them on the North/South axis.

In this spirit, *Life in Beauty* has been packaged in a beauty treasure box. You can keep the book in it or use the box for precious items. Perhaps you could place it in your desk at work and each morning take out one object to admire through the day, bringing yourself back to an awareness of beauty. I think of the old cigar boxes my grandfather used to have. To begin with, they were filled with his precious cigars. My grandmother insisted he smoke his cigars outside but he didn't mind. He would choose a cigar from his box and then step outside and enjoy time in silence. When the box was empty, he would either use it to store precious items or he would offer it to one of the grandchildren for their treasures.

Consider this to be your cigar box into which you will place things of beauty. I recently cut out a quotation from the newspaper. It goes like this:

More than kisses, letters mingle souls.
— *John Donne*

This is a perfect treasure for my beauty treasure box. So is the flat stone I picked up on the beach one day. As I hold it, I am reminded of the joy I experienced as a child while skipping stones on the water. Then there are the earrings that belonged to my grandmother. In my mind's eye, I can see her wearing them.

In traditional societies, talismans were highly valued. Each individual imbued these

precious items with meaning. This is your opportunity to do the same. Remembering how the Cree language works, when you hold a talisman you animate it and all its meaning comes alive. Sacred items were usually wrapped in red and stored, brought out for ceremonies and gatherings. Similarly, treat your objects as sacred. You will feel enormous inspiration when you hold them. They will support your *Life in Beauty*!

Sources

A Course in Miracles. Mill Valley, CA
  (Foundation for Inner Peace) 1992

Davis, Ann. *The Logic of Ecstasy*. Toronto, ON
  (University of Toronto Press) 1992

Hawkins, David R. *Power Vs. Force*. Carlsbad,
  CA (Hay House, Inc.) 2002

McLuhan, T.C. *Touch the Earth*. New York,
  NY (Promontory Press) 1971

Tolle, Eckhart. *A New Earth*. New York, NY
  (Dutton) 2005